Up Cripple Creek

A Journey To Immobility

by

Jon McVey

Published by
Wobbly Man Press
www.facebook.com/wobblymanpress

ISBN Number: 9781700363084

PREFACE

This account is the absolute God's honest, cross my heart true-ish story of my slow journey from athletic superbeing to Stephen Hawkins' physical and intellectual doppelgänger. Perhaps I'm overselling this, the reality is that this journey started when I was an average man with a lovely family and thinning hair and I write this book as an average, slightly overweight, middle-aged man with a fantastic family and little hair, with limited mobility, a wheelchair and a propensity to fall over. When I say middle-aged, I am assuming that I will live to be at least 110, well so far so good. If you have the mistaken belief that increased intellectual ability might compensate for a physical impairment, I am living proof that it does not.

Daniel Moynihan, an American politician, once said "Everyone is entitled to his own opinion, but not to his own facts." which is fine so long as you can agree on what the facts are. I admit that not every word of my account is accurate, and I may have shuffled a few events and used two half-truths to make a truth. In any case, reality is mostly subjective, even what you hear or see isn't as objective as you think.

Millions of people shared an image of a dress on the internet. Half could see with their own eyes that it was black and blue while the other half was equally convinced that the clothing they could see was white and gold. I don't know which was true. Another viral video had someone saying Yanny, for some strange reason that I really can't fathom many people could only hear them saying, Laurel. The Laurel hearers were wrong; there is nothing wrong with my hearing. Imagine a court where the word guilty as well as any reference to guilt was replaced with the word Yanny, and not guilty with Laurel. I think it would make convictions more black and white, or at least gold and blue. If my wife Diane wrote about the same events, it would be a completely different book and the words grumpy, old and git would appear with much higher frequency.

I will also admit that in my account, I may not have always observed some apparent facts. As Diane knows to her eternal frustration, I don't see things under my nose. I was once a juror doing my civic duty amongst 11 other jurors listening to the opening prosecution speech. I diligently took copious notes but unfortunately failed to notice that the prosecuting barrister was my neighbour. In my defence, I had never seen him wearing a wig before. The judge dismissed the jury, and I was summoned sheepishly back into the court. Fortunately, the judge, the court and even the defendant saw the funny side.

On occasions, I have realised that my recollection of some critical facts is incomplete. In these circumstances, I have looked to Mr Trump for inspiration, and I have filled these gaps with "alternative facts" and made something up, usually taking the opportunity to paint myself in a better light. If by chance, anyone has evidence to the contrary, they can keep their fake news to themselves.

From time to time, I will rant about something that particularly gets up my nose, and this happens quite a lot. Although there is legislation and over 11 million people with a disability in the UK, with a spending power of over £80bn, there are many short-sighted organisations that make unnecessary barriers. It baffles me that big organisations with the resources to make simple changes do unthinking things, such as a bank that wouldn't let me open a new account without visiting my inaccessible local branch, not for reasons of fraud protection or account security but to watch a sales video.

This book isn't an encyclopaedia of disability. My journey to this position started in my 30s and has been very gradual. I don't have a greater understanding of what it would be like to be deaf, blind or even losing the use of my legs in a traumatic life-changing event.

There are certain areas of life that I have no intention of including. There are matters of personal hygiene that you won't want or need to hear about, and I'm certainly not writing 50 Shades of Purple. Purple is the chosen colour for disability. I have no idea who decides the colours, but it strikes me that any new causes, ideas, political parties or movements have to select from the few remaining colours. They would have to make do with Proud Peacock, Kiwi Crush or another colour from the Dulux colour chart.

My life has gone in many directions; a few worked for and others unexpected. At different times in my life, I have imagined many ways that my fortunes could turn, both good and bad, but there was never a moment that I considered the possibility of life in a wheelchair. The direction has been unexpected, but I might as well enjoy the journey.

My family have been the unintentional partners on my journey. My gorgeous wife Diane, as well as being a constant support, has had to pick up the pieces when I have fallen, sometimes literally, and throughout she has kept me laughing. My children have grown up with my mobility becoming progressively limited. Daniel can remember me playing football with him. Emily only recalls me walking with a stick. They have learned a sort of resilience through, at times, being young carers and managing situations with a calmness beyond their years. I am also lucky to have the support and encouragement from a close family, as well as wonderful friends.

Without a place called the NeuroMuscular Centre, my life would be very different. I would unhesitatingly recommend it to anyone with muscular dystrophy or other muscle conditions. However, I have included very little about it in the book. It is a place full of lovely people and remarkable characters, and stories to fill many bestselling books, but those are their stories.

The environment at the NeuroMuscular Centre, by design, has no barriers to what you can access, whether you use a wheelchair, scooter, crutches, sticks, are a carer or a member of staff. When you strip these barriers away, you are just left with people, from all ages, backgrounds and experiences. The Centre is a big community. As people use the centre for many years, it is more like an extended family.

Almost universally, the professionals who have supported me have been empathetic and helpful, with the very definite exceptions of a social worker and an endocrinologist, but perhaps I didn't see their best sides. There isn't a professional that I have regularly seen who at hasn't done their job with the care and skill you would hope for, and almost universally I would unhesitatingly recommend the NHS services that have given me support and care over the years. In this book, I have changed names because I have amalgamated characters and tweaked stories and unintentionally I wouldn't want to infer anything that could question their professionalism.

INTRODUCTION

My plans never included using a wheelchair. It wasn't even part of plans B, C or D. Perhaps it was an eventuality that was worthy of some consideration. After all, there are, according to NHS England, 800,000 regular wheelchair users, so the odds are more than one chance in 100. If I were to win the lottery, I know precisely how I would spend the money. Half on self-gratifying high living and profligate hedonism and then I'd probably blow the remainder. However, if I played every lottery game for sixty years, there is still only one chance in 2,000 that I would have a big win.

For the first 40 years, the odds were in my favour, well I thought they were. I didn't know it, but many years before this, my destiny had already been set. Deep in my muscles, something had triggered a chain reaction of proteins and biochemicals that were gradually eroding my muscle cells. This was happening without any awareness on my part. Even when some symptoms were apparent, they didn't seem significant.

I have a muscle-wasting condition. One of numerous neuromuscular diseases, all rare and are generally given the name Muscular Dystrophy. Apparently, my condition, like some others, is technically not a dystrophy because it differs at a cellular level even though it has similar symptoms and outcomes. Well, the upshot is that my muscles are slowly wasting away. The fascinating thing is that they are affected at different rates, so how it affects life changes over time. While it affects my skeletal muscles, heart muscle and sphincter muscles are unaffected, something that my wife is very grateful for. As my condition progresses over many years, I know that next year I am likely to be much the same as I now, apart from some adaption or new way of doing things.

I should explain that I can walk, only a few metres with the help of ankle splints and two sticks. Still, it is enough to make life considerably more manageable. I don't use a wheelchair around the house, I can move between seats, all raised and with arms so that I can get up. It does provide a little exercise. The downside is that I fall. In fact, I fall quite a lot, I must have had a few hundred falls by now. I'm also slow, very slow, snail-pace slow.

Out of the house, I use a wheelchair because it is safer, I can go further and faster. I can drive and to be able to skirt around my car to the hoist in the boot is a great help in keeping some independence. For a few people, the sight of me standing up from a wheelchair seems challenging to get their heads around. Despite taking five minutes of pushing and heaving to get up, it is as if they have witnessed a miracle.

Today I can do the same things as I could yesterday. My abilities degenerate very gradually. When I look at what I could do a year ago, I can see how things have changed.

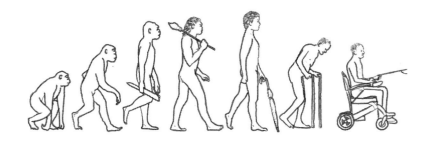

CHAPTER 1

UP CRIPPLE CREEK

"Open the door for the nice cripple" the old lady instructed the young girl. As I shuffled at my average sloth-like speed through the door, I smiled and thanked the girl and nodded to the old lady.

I laughed to myself. Cripple? That was the first time I'd been called a cripple. In the lexicon of non-PC words, I suspect cripple is relatively high, one of those forbidden words.

I suppose though the description was entirely accurate. The Oxford English Dictionary defines a cripple as; "a person who is unable to walk or move properly through disability or because of injury to their back or legs." I have a condition where my muscles are gradually wasting and the way I walk aided by walking sticks and ankle splints is slow, hesitant and ungainly.

I have no insight into the thoughts of the old lady, but I'm sure she had no intention to demean me. More likely, she was motivated by kindness and to instil in the young girl the importance of a kind gesture.

Perhaps she was mischievous in the way some old people are and as I hope to be if I get to be her age. She would know that later that afternoon the girl would recount her adventures of seeing a cripple, doubling her pocket money on a slot machine, playing smoking with candy cigarettes and eating sherbet monkey dust, to her exasperated parents.

Through the door was the doctor's waiting room. I registered my presence on the machine and looked for a seat. Many that were empty but none of these were any use to me. I could sit on them, or drop clumsily onto them, but the problem would come when my appointment was called, and I would have no chance of getting up. In the corner of the waiting room were three comfortable chairs with sturdy arms provided by the local Rotary club for the use of elderly and infirm, but these were occupied. The digital scrolling sign said that there was a 40 minute waiting time. I could ask the occupants of the comfortable chairs to move, but they might need the arms. I simply wasn't able to stand for 40 minutes. I realised not for the first or last time that I was up Cripple Creek.

There is a real Cripple Creek just west of Colorado. A neighbouring creek, although much more disagreeable, would be the ideal location for a paddle hire business. Many years ago, a rancher was building a shelter for his cows. His hapless helper accidentally discharged a gun, this was the wild west after all, and shot the farmer through the foot. Either the gunshot or the swearing farmer not unnaturally frightened a calf, who ran off and tried to jump the local creek. The unfortunate calf didn't make it and fell, breaking its leg. The rancher presumably shot his helper and named the stream Cripple Creek.

Cripple Creek gained notoriety in 1890 after a cowboy named Bob Womack found some gold. Bob obviously wasn't able to keep this good fortune quiet as he was quickly followed by 55,000 other prospectors, together with numerous saloons and brothels, happy to relieve them of any new-found wealth.

In the UK we also have plenty of place names that wouldn't pass a political correctness test. There is Cripplegate, Cripple Hill, Cripple Style. Also, Lamehill and Lamecock, although perhaps that is a reference to a different issue. In Warminster, there is Limpers Hill Mere and Withered Heath in Swindon. There is Stick Hill, Walker, Crutch Lane, Scooters End and Access Road. Besides you could visit Rickety Nook, Ricketts Close, lots of Infirmary Roads, Sickly Croft, and Limpsfield.

Having realised that I am a cripple, I thought that perhaps I should do a bit of research. I wondered if cripple was the right word, maybe I was handicapped, or an invalid. I looked online for words that people with disabilities dislike. I don't think that the list was made in any way scientifically, but unsurprisingly all of these terms came pretty high on the list. Cripple was at number 7, handicapped number 5 and invalid at number 4, above them were some unpleasant terms which were solely conceived to demean. Many of the words were made with the best intentions, sometimes to replace words that were seen as offensive before becoming offensive themselves. Meanings changes over time, words acquire connotations that were not originally intended, and attitudes develop. So for any word, over time, there is a sort of inflation in offensiveness.

If you were disabled in Saxon times, you would probably have been called a "Krupel." Even at this time, it was an old word derived from a Proto-Germanic language, so similar words were found across Europe from Norway to Italy. The term "Cripple "was first recorded as early as 950 AD.

At the time when King Cnut was debating with the tides over their right to cover his beaches, Herman the Cripple was enlightening Germany by translating Muslim scientific texts, far in advance of anything in the western world.

Herman was born in 1013, and he very probably had Spinal Muscular Atrophy although diagnosis a thousand years later is a bit hit and miss. His parents couldn't look after him, so he was taken in by Monks. He obviously thrived with their care, and although he was immobile and his speech could hardly be understood, he was a bit of a genius.

He became a monk, and they made a unique chair for him, which could be carried around. Herman got to work and wrote *Qualiter multiplicationes fiant in abbaco*, an explanation of how to do multiplication and division, with the added complication of doing it entirely in Roman numerals. This was followed by other treatises on geometry and mathematics. Through his translations he introduced pieces of equipment to the West that had been developed by Arabic scholars including the astrolabe (a forerunner of the sextant). Without this equipment, a few hundred years later, Columbus would have sailed in circles and never discovered America.

Herman also wrote about board game strategies, lunar cycles, and a historical chronicle. On top of this, he composed music and poetry, much of which still exists. He even wrote a smutty poem for the nuns at Buchau about the eight deadly sins. The imaginative nuns had discovered a new iniquity to add to the previous seven.

Herman died aged 40, but even this fatal impediment didn't stop him performing a few miracles, and 800 years later he was made a saint in 1863. Even now, this persistent monk is still about, or at least the top of his skull is. It is kept as a holy relic in Altshausn, Germany.

The year Herman was made a saint was during the height of the American Civil War and coincided with the foundation of the Hospital for the Ruptured and Crippled, the oldest orthopaedic hospital in the USA. The publication doctors would turn to would be "The Cripples' Journal" until it changed its name in 1968. What had been seen as an entirely correct descriptive word had started to be regarded as offensive.

Others have also appropriated the term. The Crips are a gang that you really don't want to meet. Based in Southern California, it is one of the most significant street gangs in the United States, in fact, it is more of an association of street gangs with an estimated 30,000 or more members. Naturally, to maintain the gang credentials, they involve themselves in murder, robbery, drug dealing, and pimping. Gang members carry canes around to display their "pimp" status. Rivals saw an opportunity for an easy insult and began calling them cripples. Being bad boys and to the discomfort of their opponents, the gang happily adopted what was intended as an insult as their badge of honour. Gang members devised a dance called the Crip Walk to display their affiliation. Your best chance of seeing a Crip's best moves was after they had shot you. Despite being banned from being shown on MTV because of its sinister connections, the step was frequently referenced in rap songs and quickly spread worldwide. In doing so it left much of its roots behind, in the same way as you don't need to be a bullfighter to do the Tango, there apparently is no longer a need to shoot people to do a lovely Crip Walk. If you search for Crip Walk on youtube there are numerous videos, sometimes it is now called the C Walk, presumably a little more politically correct. The move involves fast footwork, and the result is engaging and surprisingly beautiful. Done well the dancer's torso floats above their legs which appear to go their own way. Freeze frame a Crip Walk at any point, and it looks as if they have just stumbled and are about to fall so I can see how people like me could have influenced the style.

Military history is not littered with people who started their careers with physical disabilities, although many more finished their careers disabled. War is a health and safety nightmare, with all those bombs and bullets flying around, it's not surprising that many suffer life-changing injuries.

Hôtel National des Invalides is a massive and beautiful complex built by Louis XIV in 1670 as a home and hospital for aged and unwell soldiers. At the time France was in a brief period of calm after the War of Devolution where they had briefly overrun the Spanish Netherlands but been forced to hand much of the territory back. Shortly afterwards in 1672, they were at war again and so presumably the Hotel was pretty full of wounded French soldiers.

In Britain, when Henry VIII had dissolved the monasteries, the country lost the hospitals and expertise to treat war veterans. In 1682, King Charles II decided his French allies had an excellent idea, and so he commissioned Sir Christopher Wren to build the Royal Hospital Chelsea to care for veteran soldiers "broken by age or war". By the time it opened 10 years later Britain had decided it didn't like the French any longer and the subsequent war provided plenty of wounded British veterans to fill the 476 places.

From Victorian times if you were confined to a bed or couldn't leave home because you were ill or disabled, you would have been called an Invalid. Many cookbooks had a section for invalid cookery, mutton broth would build you up whether you had flu or were quadriplegic. Again the term invalid became seen as the opposite of valid, and people began to see it as offensive.

In 1504, the streets were filled with disabled war veterans, so King Henry VII passed legislation allowing the disabled veterans with their "cap in hand" to beg for money in the streets. And thereby originated the term "handicap" and a good reason why disabled people find the term insulting and patronising. Well, it would be except that this entomology is entirely wrong. Handicap was actually first recorded in 1653 as the name of a bartering game. By 1754 it was applied to horse racing where horses carry different weights to even out the field and make betting more exciting. In 1915 it was first used in the context of someone bearing a heftier burden than usual and applied to physically disabled children, slowly extending to include adults. Handicapped comes top of the list of words that people with disabilities detest.

Disability isn't a new term. From the 1640s disability was defined as incapacity in the eyes of the law. By the 1980s "handicapped" was gradually replaced with "disabled" which coincided with new ways of thinking about disability. The prefix "dis" usually applies to negative things, so some groups have started using forms that emphasise the ability part such as "dis-ability" or "disAbility"

The comedian Adam Hills has a part of his leg missing and in an interview with the Guardian in 2012, declared "mutant" a much better word than "disabled". "It sounds so much cooler," he said. Likewise, for many, cripple has been re-appropriated, and members of the disability rights movement have reclaimed words such as "cripple", "crip", and "gimp" to refer to themselves.

Perhaps there should be a name more relevant to my condition. I like fall meister, after all, if you wish to make any word sound hipster cool just follow it with meister. There are places in this world where you can probably pay the price of a small house for a small cup of coffee made by a barista meister or have a few hairs trimmed from your beard by a barber meister.

Norman Wisdom is deserving of the accolade of fall meister. If you are under 40 you or not from Albania you may not be aware of Norman Wisdom. At the peak of his career in the 1950's and 60's he was one of Britain's best-known stars, famous for shouting "Mr Grimsdale" and spectacularly falling over any step or obstacle. Always a joker he even tripped when he was knighted by the Queen, hitting the ground and recovering to standing in the same fluid motion. As his fame gradually faded in the UK, his gentle slap-stick humour became a sensation in communist Albania. Unfortunately, I don't fall with any more style than a big bag of jelly.

Looking at things a different way, there are two aspects to disability, the actual condition and the environment. If you put me on the top of a mountain with two sticks, I would be in big trouble, yet in a shopping centre with a power chair, I can do the same things as anyone else. In fact, in a shopping centre, my disability is of no consequence, I am not any less able (or disabled) than anyone else. As my family have discovered, I can carry an awful lot of shopping on my knee, so in that respect, I am more able than average. That is until some planning idiot places bollards that are too narrow to go through. Disability is perhaps more about the environment than the medical impairment. Unfortunately, the barriers are not only physical but in people's attitudes to disability.

Language has changed, but I'm not sure that the attitudes of Herman's fellow monks were any less enlightened. I am much more disheartened by some attitudes than worried about the language people use. It is more irritating to be ignored or left out or for people to ask Diane about me in my presence. Personally, I don't mind when people ask me about my condition, but a few are disarmingly direct. Although if their questions are intrusive, they seldom hang on long enough for me to get to a full description of my toileting arrangements. I'm also frustrated by a few businesses that lack the forethought to provide information or make simple changes that would enable me to purchase their products. That is not to say that language isn't significant, businesses and organisations should care about the language they use, it says something about their values.

In the doctor's surgery, one of the armchairs was occupied by a young man with a plastered ankle and crutches who struggled to stand up and offered his seat. Warmed by this act of generosity, I couldn't accept his offer. His need was at least as big as mine. Well I thought it was until I realised that his name had been called, so I thanked him and dropped down in the chair with a delicate bang

Being in a wheelchair avoids this problem, but there are still times when life takes you down Cripple Creek, along Disability Ditch, up Invalid Inlet, flushed along Lame Drain, and sluiced down Handicapped Hole without a paddle or other mobility aid.

CHAPTER 2

DIAGNOSIS

It's not every day that you grow a pair of clowns feet. Taking my daughter Emily to school that was precisely what, inexplicably, appeared to have happened. As I stepped out of the car, pains shot through my feet as if a size 36 foot had been squeezed into my already oversized size 12 shoes. It wasn't the pain though that led to my diagnosis of clown's feet, I could think of several reasons why my shoes could be suddenly the cause of excruciating agony. After all, they were old, worn and mistreated. Having difficulty finding shoes to fit, I tended to wear comfortable pairs until the soles wore through or the stitching fell apart.

What was odd about today was the way I walked. I had parked a few hundred yards from the school entrance. Taking my daughter's hand, we strolled down the pavement. Just behind me, I could hear "slap, slap, slap". Assuming our slow progress was delaying a parent impatient to drop off their child, so they could get to work on time, I stopped and moved to the side. I was surprised to find there was no one there, so we continued our progress. "Slap, slap, slap" It started again, and when I stopped, it stopped, and gradually I realised that it was my feet flapping against the pavement.

The more I tried to walk normally, the weirder it got. I had forgotten how to walk. With each step, my feet flapped down on the pavement in a way that would look the most natural (if clowns are in any way natural) in a pair of red and white clowns shoes. I flapped my way down to school and back.

Returning home, I immediately searched and found a pair of size 13 shoes on eBay. An extra size bigger seemed like a good idea. When you get to size 13 there isn't much choice, and most of what there is are in the weirdest styles, you are more likely to find yellow suede creepers, 4-inch stilettos or purple brogue winkle pickers than a pair of plain comfortable men's shoes. Fortunately, I found something suitable, and in due course, they arrived. I was pleased to discover that they were cosy, if a little tight, but that often happens with new shoes. They were comfortable until I stood up and tried to walk. The shoes felt much too small again, with each step my foot loudly slapped onto the floor and but worse than that, I had forgotten how to walk. I had walked for well over forty years, and it was something that happened without thought. I only had to think that I want to get somewhere and my legs and feet would pretty much sort it out, clambering over obstacles, and climbing steps without having to bother my brain for further instructions. They would complain if they'd been asked to go too fast or too far, but they would still work. Now for some reason, they had forgotten everything and to walk I had to think about each action of my legs. Lift the knee, lean forward, move the foot forward until it makes contact with the ground. I could do it, or rather I could stomp around, but it felt and looked like Frankenstein's Monster before he had much practice.

This was the point that I realised that I should see the doctor. This wasn't the first symptom, in fact looking back, I had symptoms for 10 or 20 years and possibly more, but it was the first symptom that I couldn't discount as getting older or just some unusual quirk of my body.

"Ready, steady..", I had foolishly entered a Father's Day race at my daughter's school sport's day. I had assumed that it would be a running race, but as I stood with the other athletic-looking fathers on the start line the headteacher informed us that it wasn't a running race and only hopping would be allowed. She could have mentioned that before, I never liked hopping much. By the time the headteacher shouted "GO" most of the fathers were halfway down the hall. On the starting line, I was frantically bobbing up and down with no effect like my foot was nailed to the floor. Whatever I did, I couldn't move. I had advanced about four inches by the time every other father had finished hopping the length of the hall and back. Being one of the two oldest parents I hadn't expected to come anywhere better than second to last, but I had hoped to have gone further than four bloody inches. Then I fell over. Crestfallen and crushed, I accepted total defeat. The upsides were that Emily was playing with her friends, and Diane wasn't there to see my unmitigated failure. A group of young mothers came over to see if I was alright, so I played on things a little and enjoyed their attention. I decided that perhaps you can forget how to hop.

I made an appointment with our local General Practitioner, and within a few days, I was sitting in a consulting room with a young locum doctor. I found it surprisingly difficult to explain my problem, it is relatively easy to describe a sprained wrist or uncomfortable piles, but demonstrating something odd about the way I walk I assumed that I would be sent off with an appointment to see the mental health team. The doctor got me to walk a few times across the room and then confessed that she had no idea. She thought that a specialist might have more insight, but she couldn't decide which specialist my symptoms would interest, so she covered the odds and sent me to an endocrinologist and a neurologist.

I first saw the endocrinologist at a hospital that I have not been to before or since. I explained that I had been sent to see him as well as a neurologist. He seemed a bit annoyed that this violated some etiquette and sent me away, saying that I should decide on one specialist to see. I found this statement very puzzling, did he think I had dropped by on a passing impulse? Well, that was a waste of time.

My next visit was to a neurologist at a local hospital. I was summoned into the room where a small elderly lady sat behind a large desk. She poked me, hit bits with a reflex hammer and asked questions about my sex life. She sat back in her chair and told me that there was something wrong. I wondered what she thought, she replied;

"Let's wait until we get the test results."

And she sent me for a raft of tests. The first was called an evoked potential test which involved sitting in front of a computer screen with a moving chequerboard pattern while wearing a cap fitted with electrodes. The operator explained that its use was to diagnose Multiple Sclerosis.

A few days later, I had an appointment for an MRI scan of my brain and spinal cord. Diane and I sat in the waiting room and watched "Homes under the Hammer" playing on the TV. There was no sound, but it made no difference, having seen the programme we knew precisely what was being said. Martin Roberts was having a seizure because some bastard had covered the ceiling with Artex. There followed a selection of views of ceilings so "Dancing on the Ceiling" or another ceiling themed song will have been playing in the background. It then cut to the auction, with a few bored-looking bidders and one excited looking couple, who were ultimately the successful bidders. It turned out they were a couple of half-wits who had bought it on an impulse without reading legal pack. Unfortunately, I will never know whether the house fell down before they managed to hang some wallpaper because I was called in for my MRI.

The MRI scanner is a big white machine with a hole in it. I lay on a table and was given a set of headphones. The operators sitting in a glass room looking down on the machine. The table was automatically manoeuvred in and out of the hole. My job was to lie still and follow instructions. The hole is just big enough to fit into with an inch or two to spare, my shoulders and toes touched the sides. I used to enjoy caving, and so I was comfortable with the confined, claustrophobic space. I couldn't help but wonder what happens when a thirty stone person needs an MRI scan. I was most fascinated by the noise. The reason for the headphones became clear. MRIs clatter, whirr and bang in a way that you would expect from a Victorian steam engine rather than an ultra-high-tech machine. The table moved in and out of the hole and from time to time, the operators re-entered the room to change my position or to put a further contraption over my head.

A few days later, I was called by the neurologist. She explained that there were problems with the evoked potential results, but there was nothing on the MRI scan. I relayed the information to Diane that my brain scan had found nothing, Diane helpfully responded that she could have told them there was nothing to see. The neurologist's tone changed and was quite upbeat. There is an anomaly in your blood test, however, your CK levels are very high. She stated that this was something she hadn't expected, but I still wondered why the upbeat tone. It wasn't until much later that I realised that this information suggested a much better prognosis. This was an indication that it might not be the more likely diagnosis of motor neurone disease or multiple sclerosis.

The neurologist went onto explain that she would need to refer me to another Consultant who was a muscle specialist, but before that, she sent me for an electromyograph. In 1870, Eduard Hitzig stuck needles into an exposed dog's brain and discovered when he connected them to an electric current it caused involuntary leg movements and muscle contractions in the unfortunate animal. I don't know what happened to the dog, but I suspect that it was considering a similar experiment into the consequences of sinking his teeth into Eduard's testicles. These experiments were done at Eduard's home because the University of Berlin, not a place that I would associate with sentimentality, decided that this was going too far. The electromyograph works in the same way, plunging long needles into various muscles to intercept and shock the nerves. Considerably more preferable to the treatment of the unfortunate dog, but needles and electricity were not something I was looking forward to. I have an aversion to pain.

We sat amongst other nervous-looking people in the waiting room, one by one they disappeared down the corridor, reappearing half an hour later looking downcast and broken. In time it was my turn, and I went into a small room with an examination table and an old looking computer attached to a couple of long wires. These would be attached to the needles.

A glum-looking doctor skewered my legs and arms with the long thin needles, but each time he wasn't content until he had twisted and prodded. At some point and for an unfathomable reason, he was happy that the needle was in the right place. To be fair, the experience wasn't as painful as I had feared, but I made sure for the sake of those waiting, to look downcast and broken as I re-entered the waiting room.

A few weeks later, we sat in another waiting room, waiting to see the Muscle Specialist. He obviously thought I was someone notable as he came out to meet me although Diane noticed that he was watching me walk to his consulting room. Inside four other people were sitting at the back of the room. He explained that they were medical students and asked for my permission for them to sit in. The Consultant (Doc) was an amiable man, with the ability to put us at ease with a casual joke and an air of professional competence. In fact, he still is amiable as I still see him every six months or so. He put out three fingers and asked me to squeeze them. I did this, but he could easily unpeel them one by one to release the grip. "That's good," he said and then turned to the students to explain something in unintelligible medical vocabulary.

"I can tell you what is wrong with you." This was exciting news. It had taken about a year to get to this point, and I had now collected lots of hints and comments from my many doctor's visits and tests. Trying to research these and make sense of the symptoms on Google was fruitless. I couldn't find a condition, apart from Hypochondria, that didn't match my symptoms.

"I can tell you what you have, the good news is that it won't kill you, although you need to take care with your swallowing and falling" Doc explained, "but it will be a pain in the arse, a real pain."

Doc went on "You have inclusion body myositis", I heard "You have inc.... blah, blah, blah" I hoped that he would repeat the name he told me. He did repeat it, but still, my brain couldn't retain the words. Fortunately, he said that it is usually called IBM. Ah, at last, a simple acronym, what's more one that shares with a major international company. If Diane hasn't remembered the name, or the acronym, I should be able to search for it on the internet.

I used to regularly go to meetings in London with an organisation that loved acronyms. I mean they really loved acronyms. The chair could happily preside over a whole meeting uttering nothing else but acronyms.

"The DoH under s64 paid for study." The Chair would start. At this point I was OK, I was well aware of Section 64 funding that Department of Health.

"We appointed the bra for the frog." She continued. I had stepped into a parallel universe where that sentence made sense and where amphibians had their modesty preserved. She appeared surprised at my ignorance and responded patiently that the Behavioural Research Agency undertook the research of the Family Research Open Group.

"and the HNC said that it was a big 6S" she continued

By this point I had decided to beat my head against the table, but instead I butted in "I'm sorry for my ignorance. Are you talking about Higher National Certificates and what is 6S?"

Recognising that I had some form of severe mental impairment, she spoke slowly "the AGENCY said that it was a big SUCCESS."

That evening, when Diane and I got home, I went to my laptop to find out what I could about my condition. I opened up Google and typed in ICI and muscle. The first result was a link about sphincter muscles that didn't look right, and the following results looked equally unpromising. I tried other organisations ICI, ICL, IMI, IRS, IXL with equal lack of success. At this point, I did what I do when I have exhausted all logical paths and resorted to asking Diane who immediately put me on the right track.

Even though Doc had made a diagnosis, there were more tests to be sure that it wasn't a different condition. Because my feet appeared to have grown, they also needed to rule out Padget's disease, a condition where bones continue to grow and sometimes accompanies IBM. So in the following months, I had a biopsy and numerous appointments with a range of specialists. Having a rare condition makes you particularly attractive to some doctors. I think that some want to collect as many rare diseases on their books, a bit like trading cards. They would add me to their list just so they could swap me with a case of Moebius Syndrome.

CHAPTER 3

HOW DID THIS HAPPEN?

I hadn't used Facebook much, but I quickly discovered that I could join groups and communicate with others that have the same condition. There is some sort of innate need to find people who share the same experiences and gather information, it's very comforting to know that others have found ways to cope. Whatever medical condition you have, there will be a Facebook group. Having just written this, I thought I ought to check my facts, and yes, there is a group for people with Haemorrhoids. There is even a group for people with Halitosis, but as it only has one member, I'm not sure that you can call it a group. That seems a little sad. Halitosis sufferers join the group, you are not alone.

IBM can be inherited, but the type I have is called sporadic IBM, which, as was explained to me, means no one knows why some people get it. It was probably some environmental factor that triggers a response in some cells, that in turn triggered a response in muscle cells which triggers further cells creating a domino effect, spreading through all my muscle cells.

Unfortunately, no one knows what the trigger is. It seemed like a critical question following my diagnosis, after all, if it affected me could it affect others exposed to the same environmental factor, my wife and children.

It seems that this is a question that naturally interests most people with IBM. If you know the cause, there is the possibility of prevention. This was a question posed on one Facebook group that got many responses from people across the world. Smoking seems like an obvious candidate, as it is a risk factor for so many conditions. I was dumb enough to smoke for a while until my early twenties. Very few of the group had ever smoked so even if it was a risk factor, there must be other things at play.

It could be that we have all had a specific viral infection at some point. I pondered whether it could be something pigeons carry. I worked in an office that had a constant battle with feral pigeons. Despite a fake owl, a real falcon and spikes fitted to everything, the gutters filled with pigeon excrement every few weeks. On wet days the gutters would overflow, and the only way to enter or leave the building was through a shower of diluted pigeon shit. I couldn't find anything on Google that people catch viruses from pigeon guano, besides there have probably been millions of other possible vectors that could have carried a virus.

I found out that there are three people in my small home town with IBM. This seemed like a bit of a coincidence. When I asked Doc if this was significant, he laughed and responded: "So you're not the only gay in the village." If any items are spread about totally randomly, there are areas where there are none and others where there are several. Having three people with IBM in one place is probably random coincidence and is not evidence of a cluster.

Another favourite contender amongst the group were statins, although it was immediately evident that this can't be the only cause as very many of the group didn't take them. Others like myself were prescribed statins after being diagnosed with IBM. The vast majority of people are over 60 when they are diagnosed with IBM, which coincides with the age people start using statins, so it is not surprising that many people's first symptoms occur at about the same time. Perhaps they have conflated two things that have no connection. A possible side effect of statins is muscle inflammation which only adds smoke to the fog.

There was one group of responses that did catch my attention. There were some veterans from the Vietnam war who blamed their IBM on exposure to Agent Orange. One mentioned a memory of being covered in blisters. It reminded me of a date I had as a young man, I was working at a festival and had been in a group clearing a piece of hillside. Someone and something had been there before us, and it looked like no-man's-land in the battle of the Somme. The brown ground where nothing was living was covered with pieces of dead conifers and scrub wood. Some blisters appeared on my hand and over a week, or so, they grew until they covered much of the back of my hand and fingers. I can still see a mark where the most enormous blister eventually turned a horrible mix of yellow and green.

This was precisely the time when I had been invited to lunch with the family of someone I had been courting for only a couple of weeks. I wasn't sure how I had the good fortune to be dating her, but if these things are inexplicably determined by the astrological position of moons, planets, stars and galaxies, something was already moving out of alignment.

A few days previously I had bought some chocolates as a gift, but I ate them myself when I discovered that her brother had recently ended a relationship with the chocolatier's daughter and the brand's name was unmentionable in their household.

I arrived at the date with no gift, and I decided to conceal my unsightly pustules with long sleeves and by placing my blistered hand underneath the other. I would explain my problem before my hands were seen. Unfortunately, I hadn't considered that a father's natural instinct is to firmly shake the hand of any potential suitor. Before I was able to warn him, my hand was in his vicelike grip at which point he would have been instantly aware of the balloons of jelly-like fluid hazardously moving under his fingers. He had the remarkable good grace not to flinch or appear to notice. The rest of the date went well, apart that is, from the cotton jumper which she lent me to go for a walk and because it had gone cold. That evening

I washed it ready to return to her, but when it dried it was quite a lot smaller and had a stain where I had spilt something, so I decided when I got another paycheque I would replace it.

Over the next couple of weeks, my star sign, Taurus ascended into the china shop constellation. During this period of astrological chaos, I didn't miss an opportunity to put one foot firmly in my mouth while shooting myself in the other and so when she inevitably had the good sense to gracefully pull the rug, I didn't have a leg to stand on. I never did replace her jumper.

I went to see my GP and asked him if I could have touched some chemical used to kill the trees. He didn't know what it was, but he thought that it was probably a reaction to a plant that I had brushed up against. I didn't work with plants, so I wasn't convinced. He prescribed some antihistamine cream which seemed to work.

Apparently, many of the chemicals in Agent Orange are used in commercial defoliants used to clear scrubland. The veterans had pursued their case because if it were shown that their IBM did have a possible link to the use of Agent Orange in Vietnam, they would have been entitled to compensation. A commission had looked at the evidence behind their claim, they compared the number of veterans diagnosed with IBM to the amount you would expect to see in the population. As nearly a million young US men went to fight it is not surprising that a few of them would, in any case, develop IBM. The commission decided that it couldn't make a link.

I realised that I could make up a new theory every day. Over the years, I will have been exposed to untold numbers of metals, inorganic chemicals, organic chemicals, biochemicals, viruses, bacteria and other biological agents. In most cases, I would have been totally unaware that I had been exposed. It seems like a long shot to work out which thing was the critical agent. To me, it doesn't make any difference what the cause was. Whatever it was, the evidence is unambiguous, that others around me, even if they have been exposed to the same environmental factors, have no more chance of developing IBM than anyone else. So, I am content in not knowing what caused the cells in my muscles to start self-destructing. Perhaps someone will identify the cause, and it may help find a way to prevent others from developing IBM in the future, but at the moment who knows.

CHAPTER 4

LOVED ONES

Exploding wheelchairs is another thing to worry about. It has happened. Don't believe me, then I'll tell you the true story of Archie.

In 1943 Archibald Brown decided to get some fresh air. His nurse Doris Mitchell collected his wheelchair from the air raid shelter where it was stored. Archibald, now 47, had lost his legs following a motorcycle accident when he was 24. Dressed in pyjamas, dressing gown and covered with a travelling rug, he transferred to the chair, and together they set off. After about a mile, Archibald decided to have a smoke. As he lit the cigarette, there was a violent explosion. Poor Doris suffered leg injuries, but Archibald and his chair had disappeared. Bits of the unfortunate Archie were found at the side of the road and in nearby trees and gardens.

An investigation followed and as it was the middle of the war, the Police concluded that Archie was probably not a prime target for Nazi bombers and so enemy action was ruled out. The investigation found the surprising cause was an anti-tank mine that had been placed under the wheelchair cushion.

It further emerged that Archie was a controlling, cantankerous and aggressive husband and father. He would ring a bell and berate his wife if something was out of place. He frequently beat and humiliated his son Eric. I don't know if he became bitter after his accident or perhaps Archie was always violent and cantankerous, but his behaviour to his wife and son deteriorated when he took a liking to his new nurse. His nurse, in turn, energetically attended to Archie's needs that were not listed in her contract.

It was perhaps only a matter of time until someone snapped and decided that life could be better without being shouted at and beaten by a belligerent old sod. Eric had joined the Army, had ready access to Anti Tank Mines and had been trained in their use. Perhaps it didn't need Poirot to find a likely suspect. Eric confessed to murdering his dad and was declared insane at his trial.

Carers have a tough time. Their support is unrecognised. As a beneficiary of regular loving care from my family, I know how easy it is to forget to show appreciation. It is easy to vent frustrations at the wrong person, just because they are there. Most manage to deal with their situation better than Archie, and so, fortunately, there have been very few exploding wheelchairs.

The Rev Mary Webster knew of the difficulties of caring for elderly parents. When she was 31 years old in 1954, she left her vocation as a congregational minister to care for her ageing parents. The reality for Mary was that she lost her income and faced the prospect of poverty in her old age. But this is what dutiful daughters did in those days.

After nine years in this role, Mary wrote to the national press, highlighting the problems for single women who were effectively "under house arrest" discharging their caring responsibilities. Mary recognised that she and others in her position needed support, and this struck a chord with many, and there was a flood of letters and donations in response to the articles. It seems that Mary was onto something and had tapped into the private suffering of many who had disregarded their own needs while devotedly caring for elderly or disabled family members. Naturally, momentum rapidly gathered leading to the foundation of the carers movement. It wasn't until 1996 that the law recognised that carers have needs in their own right.

In the UK, about 6.5 million people care for someone, and there is likely to be an additional 2.5 million in 20 years. For some care might be as simple as helping with the shopping, but many are providing constant and intensive help without respite. The selfless devotion of carers saves the country a shed load of money. That is assuming we are talking about the Muratoa Stick Shed, the world's biggest wooden shed. It is estimated that it would cost £138 billion each year if they all went on strike and paid carers had to pick up the pieces.

Assuming the Government would pay this bill, perhaps they could start with the dubious £350 million that the Brexit bus alleged would become available each week. This would only amount to £18.2 billion and would hardly make a dent in balancing the books. Perhaps they could add the tax paid by massive companies, except almost one in five of Britain's most prominent companies didn't pay any corporation tax last year. They could scrap the Army, Navy and Airforce which would perhaps save another £36 billion. There would be a lot of expensive and dangerous hardware to sell, which some doggy regime would be pleased to buy. This would perhaps be sufficient to pay the first years bills, but it would probably be worth cancelling HS2 to fund the care bill for another few months.

Caring families and especially wives, get a rough deal, especially emotionally. If Diane has an appointment at the hospital and I accompany her, I'm the one who people open doors for, offer cups of tea to or ask after.

Recently, we went away for a couple of nights to stay with family. My sister had rented a barn, so it was a rare occasion for us all to have a weekend together. As we drove out of the road where we live I saw a young couple with a baby and small toddler packing every spare cubic centimetre of their car with car seats, travel cot, highchair, bags of feeding bottles, baby food, steriliser, bowls, cups and other equipment, toys, teddies and books, changing bag and a massive bag of nappies. I turned to Diane and said, "That's something I don't miss!"

Diane looked at me. "Did you just say that?" she asked incredulously. I didn't know how to answer that question as she was wearing her "don't mess with me" face. Diane pointed out that she had just packed in our boot my electric wheelchair, chargers, bed frame, walking sticks, transfer board, toilet frame, riser seat, cushions, urine bottles, tablets, Camel rising seat and pump. To say nothing of the planning involved when we go away to ensure that everything was on one level, that there is enough room to get around, that parking is nearby and isn't on gravel, that the bed is high enough and that the bathroom is suitably adapted.

Looking after me is something Diane does even when she disregards her own health needs. It must be galling when she meets someone having just returned from one of her hospital visits and is in constant pain to be asked: "How's Jon". Equally, if Diane needs care, there is little I can do to reciprocate her loving attention, and I don't stop needing help to empty urine bottles and help with unspeakable acts of personal hygiene. She also ensures that our children get all the love, care and attention they deserve. Now add in the jobs around the house and in the garden that I can no longer manage. On top of this, she also supports her elderly parents and deals with the pressures of her work. A cleaner, a handyman and at times support from care workers can alleviate some of the demands, but the costs quickly mount.

Diane has been by my side for 25 years. At the time we met, I worked for a brilliant charity, and we had just moved into a new office. I had seen Diane a few times. She was beautiful, and so I asked her and some other friends to help paint the new office. Not the most promising start, but I was smitten with her bubbly personality and sense of fun. Surprisingly afterwards she agreed to go for a meal with me. On our second date, I forgot my wallet, so it was perhaps surprising that we got as far as a third date. Despite the odds we soon became inseparable.

I proposed to Diane while we were on a boating holiday on the Norfolk Broads. Amidst the romantic backdrop of St Benet's Abbey, she agreed. It was fortunate really as the remainder of the holiday could have been really awkward. Perhaps she consented for fear of not getting a lift back. A year later, we married.

One morning while listening to the news on the radio, Diane was put out. They reported on some bloke who died ages ago had been made a saint.

"Overlooked again, where's my sainthood?" she said

I pointed out that while I value her love and help, with regards to sainthood, there were a few criteria that she didn't meet. Firstly it does help to be Catholic. More importantly, you have to be dead. She wasn't happy with this and felt it was a bit discriminatory. I also mentioned that you need to perform a miracle or two. Diane pointed out that the previous night I had been snoring so loud that the bed shook, so in many ways, it was a miracle that she hadn't put a pillow over my head.

Diane is right, she is a saint. Actually, she is more than just that. When we married, we made our vows to each other. Looking back in hindsight she really didn't have any idea what she was signing up for or understand everything living with me would involve. She has gained an intimacy with parts of my body and its functions that neither of us expected or wished for. I'm not sure that the wording of the vows was comprehensive but if the wedding ceremony had addressed finer points such as snoring or my not washing shaved whiskers down the sink, it would have lost some, or rather most, of the romance.

That was 25 years ago, and despite my few faults, this beautiful lady has faithfully stuck with me. I don't mean to make out that she is perfect, she has her own flaws. She has an annoying habit of being right and pointing it out. Gloating isn't an attractive trait. She can also be a bit short on sympathy, I can still remember her unsympathetic, actually hostile, response to a particularly bad cut I had on my hand. At the time she was in hospital just having had her appendix out or something like that, and as a loving husband, I had arrived with a magazine. Paper cuts can be very severe.

I think that being put down, perhaps this isn't a bad thing for me. If I fall, Diane is likely to call me an idiot before asking if I am OK. Diane tells me things I don't want to hear, and sometimes ignore, but more often than not, I find out the hard way that she was right. I wouldn't want this to get back to her. We have laughed through the most challenging times, and since we met, she has always been my soul mate and support.

This has been a journey with changing landscapes and seasons. It has included wrong turns and blind alleys, but also new, unexpected directions. I have lost things, but equally, there is much that I have gained. My condition has been a curse, but also an opportunity to live life differently. There have been difficult times, but there has been lots of laughter and love. As I contribute less to the family coffers, the fewer things I can do at home and the more help I need with everyday tasks. This all takes its toll, and naturally, there are times when it is overwhelming for us all. I am fortunate in having a wonderful wife who has been beside me throughout this journey, as well as having her own considerable trials.

My condition also affects the lives of my son and daughter. Fortunately, Daniel is old enough to remember the days when I would walk him to school and did the usual things fathers do, but for Emily, I had a stick even in her earliest memories. Both have experienced seeing me fall, and often injuring myself. They have never questioned the hypocrisy of my uttering words that they know they would be rebuked for voicing. Sometimes unintentionally my falls have taken away from what should be their moment. As a child, Emily broke her wrist, so we ended up at the fracture clinic. She was pleased with the coloured plaster sprinkled with glitter and the sticker that she had taken hours to choose. Then just as we were leaving the clinic, I fell, and suddenly I had demanded all the attention

From the age of 10, Emily was confidently directing strangers after I fell in a supermarket car park, telling them how they could help me and what not to do. Emily has joined the local young carers group, she understandably finds it is helpful to meet with other young people and share experiences. While there were undoubtedly things that we couldn't do with Emily and Dan, there are always options and something different, sometimes better, to replace them. Childhood is a crucial time.

I am also very fortunate to have the support of a beautiful family and good friends. They have adapted to let me get into their homes or changed plans and routines so that I can spend time with them.

Perhaps the moral to Archie's story is to appreciate the help family members and others give, recognise that caring is often a harder job that being cared for. It takes love, time and commitment. If this is too much, you don't feel much like thanking those around you and find that being demanding and belligerent works for you, make sure to check under your wheelchair.

CHAPTER 5

THE ART OF FALLING WITH STYLE

A lot of celebrities have found themselves on the front pages of the newspapers after a fall. Remember Madonna who was garrotted by one of her own dancers when he stepped on her cape at the Brit Awards, or Neil Kinnock falling on Brighton Beach before the 1983 General Election. These people know a few things, but I reckon that I know more about falling.

I know a lot about falling, it's my specialist subject. I have hundreds of falls under my belt, as many as the average stunt performer. There was a time when I was falling at least twice a week, sometimes twice a day. It wasn't that often to start with, but the frequency rapidly increased. Gradually I learned how to manage things so that I again fall less often.

A fake punch from the leading actor and a stunt performer knows how to fall with such style that the audience wants to see more, tell their friends and come back to watch the sequels. Unfortunately, I have neglected to master any finesse when I fall. Usually, it is about as elegant as dropping a sack of potatoes with the addition of some involuntary swear words.

Matthew's gospel states "If your hand or your foot causes you to stumble, cut it off and throw it away; it is better for you to enter life maimed or lame than to have two hands or two feet and to be thrown into the eternal fire."

I wish my feet knew they were under threat. There is no doubt that my right foot has been the cause of many stumbles and falls. I suppose I should cut it off. Come to think of it, my left foot has done its fair share, and if my right foot has gone, I believe that it will stumble more. Cut it off as well. Perhaps there is something in this idea. I have seen Para Olympians without any legs, running 400m on blades faster than I can stand up from my chair.

Matthew goes on to give similar advice about your eyes and hands. Many times I have misjudged the difference in height between my dropped foot and a step. I'd better be on the safe side and pluck my eyes out. I'm not sure that Matthew really knew how stumbling works, though. I have no idea how my hands could be at fault. They have sometimes suffered, when I have stumbled, in their vain attempt to save me, but I think my innocent hands are safe.

One medical reason I fall is because the early symptoms of my condition affect muscles in my leg that cause weakness in the knees and foot drop. That was the reason that my feet felt different and slapped against the ground like clowns feet. It wasn't enough that others noticed, apart from my mother, who thought that I needed a new pair of shoes. Surely shoes have to get to a pretty bad state to make a flapping sound.

The big problem with foot drop is muscle memory. If you step onto a pavement you naturally and without any conscious thought, lift your foot just high enough to clear the curb. If your toes are now a few centimetres lower than your heel, this has a disastrous consequence. The motion of your leading foot is suddenly brought to a halt, but your body is moving forward with an inescapable momentum. There is now no foot to place on the pavement to arrest your progress, and you fall like a felled tree.

Obviously, you try to adjust for your foot drop leading to an exaggerated knees-up walk, reminiscent of the Ministry of Silly Walks. Your muscle memory reminds you that you look like John Cleese or a dressage horse, but even then you still get caught out. One day my wife and I had the idea that we would like to buy a striking vase to adorn an old dresser, so we went to look at the factory shops in Stoke. It was midweek, and this remote part of town was quiet. I parked the car, and we crossed the street. The shop assistant was seldom bothered by customers and sat amongst delicately balanced shelves of fine gold-rimmed china, vases and glass. Today would be different. The stillness and quiet shattered with an ear-shattering crash, shelves precariously wobbling as a gruesomely distorted face pressed against the glass window. The curb here was fractionally higher than usual, and I had misjudged things. My legs lurched forward in a bizarre running motion and successfully deflected me from crashing into the pavement. Instead, I crashed face-first into the shop window.

Later, one summer day, I parked my car outside my office. I climbed out of the car with my walking sticks and went around to the passenger side to pick up my bag. The day before I had set up a stall at an event and I had brought a holdall with various items from the office. The holdall had a long strap so I could carry it safely over my shoulder and still use both of my sticks. Unfortunately, I had overestimated my carrying ability, I took the bag out of the car and swung it to gain enough height to get the strap over my head. As it rotated, it knocked the back of my knee. It was probably only a light touch, but it was enough to make my knee buckle, followed inevitably by my second knee and the rest of my body. With good fortune, I had parked next to bushes. Lovely soft bushes so my fall was broken. I was now lying amongst the leaves and twigs, but fortunately, I hadn't twisted or broken anything. The shrubs were soft, but they had thorns so although I wasn't in bad shape, moving was uncomfortable, each shuffle resulted in a spiky branch scraping across my back. Eventually, I managed to turn over.

Now the bushes formed a border between the car park and the public footpath, and I realised that two young women were walking down the path, one pushing a baby. They were engrossed in conversation with each other and obviously hadn't seen me fall. Now, this was a bit of a problem, I wasn't sure how they would react to a man in the bushes, so I lay quietly, better to let them pass. I now realised that I was committed, the closer they came, the worse it would look. As they approached, I could hear one of them discussing their employer who they obviously had little affection for. Then another horrific thought dawned, I was parked next to the bus stop. What if they were coming for the bus. I had never used the local buses, so I didn't have any idea of the timetable, but I expected that they weren't frequent. I could be lurking in the undergrowth for half an hour, during which time more people would arrive in the car park, and someone would be bound to see me. I wondered how to explain the situation without causing alarm. How would I explain it to the police? Fortunately, they were not waiting for a bus, so I waited for them to pass. I was now able to crawl to my car and pull myself ungracefully into the passenger seat.

In 2012 we went to the Olympic Stadium to watch preparations for the Olympics and the women's hockey. At the gates, I was approached by guides who had seen my sticks, and they guided me to a golf buggy. As I was driven to the stadium, I was told all sorts of facts, and I am not sure that they were all relevant. As the hockey pitch was at the far side of the park, I had a guided tour of the stadiums in relaxed style. Diane and the children didn't qualify for a lift, so walked behind.

In the stadium, a band played to the exhilarated crowd. Their repertoire was solely rousing patriotic songs which seemed a little unfair to the other teams. England team won well so by the end of the match we were in good spirits. I avoided the buggy so that I could walk back and inaccurately recount the facts told me on my outward journey. I could remember the numbers of visitors expected to each food outlet during the games, the cola bottle recycling machine. Unfortunately, my memories of what sports were happening in each stadium were less accurate.

We left the park after a delightful day and walked through the brand new shopping centre next to the park. Stylish shops were interspersed amongst marble walls and pavements. We looked in a few and through the windows of others. Something caught my eye in one shop, just as I realised that the perfectly smooth marble floors were not totally flat. Every now and again, there were little brass plates. They were only raised a few millimetres and were safely bevelled, but it was enough for me to catch my foot on, so I crashed to the floor. Within moments I was surrounded by centre staff and security guards. I had fallen with quite a thump, but in a minute or two, it was apparent that it was nothing serious. One of the centre staff was leaning over me and asking if I was injured in any way and what help I needed. The guards were kind and jovial. They offered help in getting up, but there was a bench nearby which was a better option for me. I rolled onto the seat, and the man sat next to me, I now knew he was the centre manager. He seemed a little unsure what to do but asked me questions to put onto his accident report form. He told me that I would be the first form they had filled out, almost as if it was an achievement. The guards by this time had nothing to do and were huddled talking to each other. Three of them formed a line, and each held up pieces of paper. The fourth guard called out 'Perfect 10s'. They laughed, and I was gratefully helped to a nearby coffee shop where we sat for a while with a drink. As this was before the diving had started, I believe that it was the first perfect 10s of the games.

The Para Olympics later that year were spectacular. Each day we would sit around the TV and watch athletic gods showing superhuman abilities. Running, athletics, swimming, what they could do was spectacular and what the same bodies couldn't do was irrelevant.

Suddenly disability became cool. At this time, I was walking with two sticks and splints, and strangely any conversations with strangers would inevitably turn to the achievements of the British Team. I have as much similarity to any of the contestants as I do to Usain Bolt, we are both tall and have covered 100m in under 10 seconds, admittedly for me in a car. It seemed that they recognised that just by walking with sticks, I was in some mysterious way was contributing to the success of Team GB.

I have fallen outside and inside my daughter's school, in the supermarket and in the supermarket car park, in the DIY store and in the DIY store car park, in lots of other car parks, outside our house and in most rooms inside.

On a few occasions, I have fallen out of our front door and ended sprawled on the paving slabs. The first time this happened, I was fortunately unhurt. I got onto all fours intending to crawl indoors so that I could use the stairs to help me up. We have lovely neighbours, and at this point, they were unaware of my condition. One walked past and cheerfully asked after Diane and the children. From my crawling position, I responded that they were all doing well. The fact that I was on my hands and knees didn't seem at all strange, or worth comment. Another neighbour saw me and came to explain that they were going on holiday and ask if we could put out their wheelie bin. I was now having a conversation with two neighbours while slowly working back to my front door on my hands and knees. We concluded our chat and I ungainly crawled through the door. It was evident that it never occurred to either neighbour that I had fallen, and no doubt returned home pondering what their crazy neighbour was doing this time.

Falling down is only part of the story. It is followed by a period waiting for the pain to subside and working out what damage I have done to myself, and sometimes to my surroundings. Then there is the small problem of getting up or getting into a chair. I did fall outside the British Museum. I had hardly touched the ground before I had been lifted to my feet. So quickly, I had no idea what was happening. We had the good fortune to be followed by a team of Rugby players.

It is heartwarming to discover the kindness of strangers. I fell in a supermarket, and a little frail old lady insisted that I take her hand to help me up. I am not a small or light man. I tried to explain that I was very grateful for her kind offer, but since my muscles wouldn't help much, it just wouldn't work. Like balancing an anvil on a toothpick, the fundamental laws of physics were not on her side. Despite looking frail, she was a tenacious old lady and kept her hand out insistently. Fortunately, two burly shop assistants came to help, and I was quickly standing on my feet. Probably on the way home the old lady, frustrated that her superhuman Hulk-like powers were unused, knocked down several lamposts and uprooted a letterbox.

When I hit the ground, it usually hurts, sometimes a lot. If I can get myself into a more comfortable position, I know that often the pain subsides in a few minutes and it is only then I can work out how much I have damaged myself. This takes a little time. If it hurt a lot, it takes much longer because my body suddenly dumps a load of adrenalin into my bloodstream resulting in uncontrollable shaking. If I have damaged something, there is a period of recuperation that can take days, or months if I have broken something serious.

I knew falling hurt me, but I was unaware of the effect it was having on my family. I had a bit of enlightenment on a visit to my GP for some blood tests. When it comes to needles, I am a little wimpy. I went into the treatment room and rolled up my sleeve. I can't make a fist so the nurse asked me to flex my muscles as much as I could. She found a vein and then said relax, you might feel a little scratch. If you want me to relax, don't tell me that you are about to thrust a needle into me, but I tried my best. "You're kidding me, call that a scratch," I thought as I flinched and tensed. Unfortunately, she hadn't hit the spot, so without removing the needle prodded around for a while but without success. After a time she got bored and decided to torture the other arm.

After the visit, I went back to my car and had just sat in the driver's seat. The doctors had recently added a pharmacy within the building. An old lady had just picked up her prescription and was making her way back to the car. She didn't notice the curb, her ankle gave way, and she fell with a sickening thud. It had all happened so quickly she didn't have any time to try and recover. It was immediately apparent that she would have hurt herself. I tried to get my sticks so that I could go to her, but within seconds several people had arrived including a doctor and the practice nurse. I couldn't offer any practical help, and the last thing they needed was an idiot joining the fall count. She had cut her head but seemed reasonably with it by the time I left the car park. I felt nauseous and upset by the sight of the poor old lady and started to understand a little about the impact my falls have on my family.

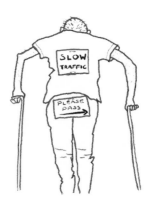

CHAPTER 6

THESE STICKS WERE MADE FOR WALKING

"Do you want to take a walking stick with you?" asked Doc. I had been talking about my falls and the pains I was having walking. I declined the offer, I didn't feel like someone who used a walking stick. I knew that I would need one, but not yet, besides I thought that it would probably mean waiting in another queue only to be given an ugly geriatric looking piece of tubing with a big grey plastic handle and oversized ferrule. I decided that the day I needed a walking stick, I would just buy one.

This day came quicker than I thought. A few weeks later, we had decided to go to the County Show. I had fallen that morning, without any injury, but it wasn't an isolated fall, I had several over the past week.

Unusually this year the Show was blessed with beautiful weather. We left the car in one of the fields that each year are co-opted as car parks and walked into the showground. The showground is very flat, but for the first time, I realised that the ground was an assortment of lumps and bumps, tufts of grass, muddy hollows, wheel ruts, sloppy cowpats and kerbs, each one a possible trap.

Diane, Daniel and Emily gradually walked ahead of me. The tables had turned, years ago when we went for a walk, Diane would walk then jog a little to keep up with me before reminding me that my legs were much longer than hers. Now they couldn't comfortably walk slowly enough, so they would naturally move ahead and wait for me. I wouldn't give any pretence of keeping up and would happily detour into each stall, to look at an animal or inspect some farm implement.

I stumbled and almost knocked into a cage of chickens. The annoyed chickens ruffle their feathers before settling again. I think that it was a lucky miss, I may have had to appease a furious farmer or worse still initiated an unfortunate chain of events. If the cage had fallen and broken open, the fleeing chicken would have run into the best of breed dog contest. The resulting chaos would have likely knocked a gate of the nearby show goats. The massive billy goats would seize the opportunity to chase the escaped nannies. The mayhem of animals in flight would knock onto other areas, and soon there would be bulls rampaging with white-coated farmers helplessly clinging to the rope attached to their harness as they are dragged through the blacksmiths display, bulldozing furnaces, which in turn ignite the marquees.

Having just averted tragedy, I saw a stall selling walking sticks. Just what I needed. Diane was clearly in favour of me buying one, but there was so much choice. We decided that a shepherds crook was a bit over the top for my needs. Many of the sticks were much too short, this is perhaps surprising as I doubt that farmers are in the main small people. After some searching, I found an adjustable metal stick that could easily be extended to the height I needed. It looked stylish, which appealed and it was the cheapest which appealed more to me.

I proudly purchased the stick and twisted the plastic collar so that the tubes could telescope to the desired length. Attached to the cane is a large plastic disk that could be screwed onto its foot. A feature that is inspired by ski poles, presumably to increase the surface area when walking over snow. I am not sure of its relevance on this sun-baked ground, but I attached it anyway. If I hadn't, perhaps I would have regretted my decision at the first crusty cowpat.

I now had three points of contact with the ground and felt immeasurably more stable. For the rest of the day, I walked confidently with my new stick, deciding whether to use my left hand or right, practising the upward flick of serious country walkers and leaning on the stick like a third leg. Occasionally I had used walking sticks for country walks, but I had never felt they were a great assistance until now. We stopped and rested by the cow stalls. The aisles were busy and narrow, so Diane and Daniel went on by themselves. Emily waited with me by the entrance. I stood with my legs a little apart resting on the stick, forming a tripod. It was all very comfortable.

Suddenly Emily started laughing and shouted "Your sinking Daddy" I was resting all my weight on the stick, exceeding the grip of the twist collar so that the walking stick was slowly collapsing and I was tipping forward. I realised the problem and managed to grab the fence, narrowly avoiding calamity for a second time.

Later that year we went to France and Disneyland. By this time, I always used a stick. It made me feel safer, especially where there were lots of people. We discovered that my stick meant we were ushered through the queues. It helped, and we happily accepted this. If you ever go to a Disney park and want to avoid the lines of impatiently waiting children and their hassled parents, I am for hire.

Over time my walking pace slowed further. A physiotherapist suggested that I use two sticks. They ordered me some, but when they arrived, they were too short. I sent them back, but they couldn't find any long enough. I am surely not the first tall person who has needed a walking stick. I searched online and bought a pair of sticks off eBay.

If your walking speed can be outpaced by an elderly sloth and you cross the road you just have to accept that sometimes you are likely to piss someone off. You hope that they are not in too much of a hurry to run you down. Plenty of drivers will wait at a crossing and eagerly beckon you to cross. I wish that I could tell them.

"You really don't know what you are letting yourself in for. Are you absolutely sure that you have the time to commit yourself to the wait? Be the way, I hold two sticks, so don't expect me to wave any thanks. At best, you might expect some weird smiling facial contortion."

As I start across the road, I notice the driver's look of realisation and disappointment. I inch forward at the speed of a three-legged tortoise with a painful corn. They had the opportunity to go but chose to be a good Samaritan. They didn't know it would mean being late for their next meeting, missing their favourite TV show or failing to make the maternity department before giving birth.

Pelican crossings bring additional pressure. They have a set crossing time, a time presumably set to allow the old and infirm to cross in ample time. I imagine that there is a group of enterprising frail OAPs who mark out a set distance in their residential home and measure the time it takes other residents to cover the length of an average crossing and sell this data to the Department of Transport.

In my town, there is a crossing at the end of the High Street. As I walked towards the traffic lights, the green man appeared, by the time I got to the edge of the pavement, it was beeping, and the little man was flashing. A white van is stopped, and the driver beckons me to start crossing. I smile and wait, but the beckoning becomes more insistent, he leans out of the window and calls "Go on mate" I try to say I'll wait, but he continues "It's OK mate, take your time" I start off across the crossing, and I have only got partway across when the green man has turned to red. The van driver continues to wave me onwards. By now the cars behind have concluded that the van has stalled and by the time I reach halfway across the road there is a continuous stream of traffic, all with the legitimate view that it was now their right of way, and besides, by the time they had seen me in front of the van it was too late to stop.

At this point my only option was to return to the original pavement and just as I reach it, the green man reappears. By now the kind van driver has realised the futility of the exercise and takes off at speed, ignoring the red light. Other pedestrians mutter their condemnation of the van driver's action. They impel me to cross again, and by the time I set foot on the crossing, the beeps have started, and the green man is flashing once more.

CHAPTER 7

FLIES

    I don't like flies, I really don't like them. We live on the edge of a small town, and our house backs onto fields. I don't know the farmer, I'm sure that he is a decent fellow and for the most part our lives don't cross. There was an incident that occurred some years ago that I feel a little guilty about. One night the old farmhouse caught alight, but fortunately, the farmer escaped to the roof and was able to call the fire brigade. Four fire tenders set up their hoses and pumped water over the house all night. The farmhouse is out of sight, and it was only the noise of the fire engines that woke me. The rest of the family slept through. I mistakenly assumed that the sound was our central heating pump. I got up, gave it a kick and went back to bed. It was lucky for the poor farmer that I wasn't his only chance of rescue.

However, there are a few occasions when country life does cross the fence and impinge on our experience. Once a year, the farmer likes to cover his field in pig manure. If you live in town you may not know that pig manure is the most pungent of all manures and as well as the smell, it makes your eyes burn. A local farmer was sued when he accidentally sprayed his pig slurry over the hedge. Unfortunately, the other side was a favourite spot for young lovers to park up. It wasn't the climax that the startled couple had hoped for, but they were lucky that they were inside the car. It appears that the burning is not just a sensation, as when the couple washed their car, which I presume was pretty quickly, the muck came off as did most of the paint.

I don't mind the smells, after all, we have the benefit of looking out over the countryside. There is one thing, however, that I could do without. The farmer sometimes puts cows in the field. When the weather is warm and wet, cow pats are the perfect breeding ground for flies. Open a window and flies will find it. Once the unwelcome little faeces footed pests are inside, they frustratingly buzz around every window, but they never discover the open one and fly out. We have tried attaching fly catching patches to the windows. The devious traps are decorated with a picture of a sunflower and are covered with a sticky substance that grips to a flies leg. As it wriggles to escape, it gets more and more stuck. Well, that's the theory, the only problem is that flies seem to know this. There could have been 10 flies on the window, they would buzz above, below and around the patch, but not one would venture over it. The sunflower was on our kitchen window for a whole year without a single kill.

Every now and again, we are visited by a horsefly, and I hate horse flies even more. They are twice as big as a housefly and even uglier. On top of that, they bite. Fresh from bathing in septic manure they sink their feted mouthparts deep into your flesh, leaving red infected swollen lumps that grow into bubonic like boils and cause agonising and irreversible swelling of your limbs. You would think that no one loves a horse fly, but I saw a biologist on the television who knew everything there was to know about them. He liked them so much that he converted his garage to breed flies of different species to study. I wondered if he had any human friends. He pointed out that it is only the female horsefly that bites, she has saw-like mouthparts which she uses to hack out a lump of flesh. She needs the protein to produce eggs and more little horse flies.

This summer my nemesis flew into our bedroom. It was our bedtime, and I didn't want its festering infectious jaws sawing chunks of flesh off my body. And oh yes, I also didn't want Diane to be bitten either.

I have to admit that I didn't know whether this was a female horse fly, but then I have no idea how to sex horse flies. In any case, it wasn't still long enough to get a good look at it. Horseflies are a lot slower than the average house fly, so I thought that I would have a fair chance swatting it. Propped up against the wall with a walking stick and a rolled magazine I thrashed about as it flew in and out of range.

Diane wasn't much help partly because the fly insisted on flying around at ceiling height and out of her reach, but mostly because she was laughing too much. Every thrust and parry seemed to increase her hilarity until her laughing seemed to be causing her physical pain. This was now a matter of honour, a duel and the odds were evens. On the one hand, I might swat the fly, on the other, I might fall. Diane pointed out that she wouldn't like to explain this to the accident and emergency team.

It flew past my face. I clipped it, and it spiralled down to the floor. I followed with a heavy swat. I lifted the magazine to see the bloody remains on the carpet, but there was nothing there. Somehow the fly was sitting on the wall watching me.

It now changed tactics. Perhaps believing that I wouldn't be stupid enough to hit myself, it sat on my forehead. It underestimated me, and I forcefully and painfully struck my head. The fly was sitting on the same piece of wall watching me.

Eventually, it settled on a window ledge, and I covered it with a glass. I put a sheet of paper under it, opened the window and shook it out. After a noble fight, perhaps it had earned the entitlement to fight another day.

CHAPTER 8

SPLINTS

Probably for thousands of years people have improvised supports out of sticks and metal to help them walk. Many consider Jean-André Venel, an 18th-century Swiss doctor as the father of orthotics. His life was certainly less controversial than the other claimant to this title. Nicolas Andry, a French medical doctor, wrote a book "L'orthopedie" that described the art of correcting and preventing deformities and likened limbs to the crooked trunk of a young tree that could be straightened "by bandaging the bent limb to an iron plate" As Professor of the College of France, Andry was very ambitious and energetic, but was also intensely disliked by his peers. It seems that many had good reason to hold a grudge. He demoted the barber-surgeons, dismissed recently created posts and mercilessly criticised the writings of his fellow doctors. It seems that Andry also had quite puritanical views and so forced everyone to strictly abstain from any festivities, fast from foods and undertake acts of penance during Lent. Disgruntled colleagues called him Worm Man after he wrote a book on parasitic worms. Weirdly this book included a chapter on sperm. In 1748, Julien Offray de la Metrie, a doctor and satirical writer, called Andry "the dishonoured father of orthopaedics".

In 18th Century Wales, Hugh Owen Thomas followed his father into the family business of broken bones repair. His father Evan had been in trouble with the law because he wasn't a trained physician, but he continued to practice. His success galled some of his competitors who had trained as doctors, so they burned down his home. However, he earned enough to send Hugh and his four brothers to medical school.

Hugh set up in practice with his father, but he was eccentric and hot-tempered, and they parted ways, and Hugh went to practice amongst the poor, prostitutes and criminals of Dickensian Whitechapel.

Hugh must have loved his work, on Sundays, he treated the poor for free, and if there weren't sufficient poor people to treat he was rumoured to have hired ruffians to break a few bones so that Hugh would have some patients to practice on.

Doc had explained that orthotics would help my gait and prevent foot drop. He made an appointment for me with the orthotics department. At the furthest point and tucked behind the mortuary, the department obviously wasn't the hospital showpiece. Inside it was no better. It was busy though, as it shared a waiting room with chiropody, dermatology and other unglamorous clinics. The reception directed me to a further waiting room, through some swing doors. I shared this room with four other waiting patients. In this group, I was the youngster, I would estimate that they all had a 30-year start on me. As I waited, another arrived, sat in a wheelchair, dressed in pyjamas and knees covered with a blanket. The porter made a cheery comment and left. The dingy waiting room also functioned as a storage area, or perhaps a museum. Haphazardly stacked around collapsed shelves were artificial legs, splints, callipers and miscellaneous cardboard boxes. They didn't look new. All wood, leather straps, rusting metal and dust, and I doubt that anything had been moved for 50 years. I found it fascinating and discomforting like some grizzly puppet theatre, looking at a pile of left legs laid across one shelf, next to a similar collection of right legs and alongside a sort of arm contraption connected to a shoulder attachment. The original owners of the limbs would have long gone, I wondered how they lost their legs and how they coped with these torturous looking limbs.

Soon I was called into another dingy room and was fitted for my own orthotics. The orthotic technician looked at my feet, asked me to stand and walk, then pressed my feet into a strange foam with the same texture as the oasis blocks that my mother used to arrange flowers. My consultant had previously told me about a silicon orthotic that would prevent foot drop but would be comfortable and inconspicuous. The technician said that my foot drop had already progressed too far.

At the next appointment, he would make a cast of my feet so they could make splints that correctly fitted. I had intended to arrive early to grab some sandwiches at the volunteer-run food kiosk, but there was a traffic jam on the motorway, so I arrived just in time and hungry. The technician said that he would put a tubular bandage over my feet, then make a plaster cast and finally cut it off in a line down the front. Unfortunately when it came to do it the roll of tubular bandage ran out, so grumbling the technician went off in search of a new box. Half an hour later, he returned without a dressing, but with a roll of cling film, he had purloined from the food kiosk.

"I wish people would replenish things they use, I spend half my time restocking this place" the technician griped. "It doesn't matter, though, I'll use another technique that I developed."

He moisturised my leg and then wrapped it tightly in cling film. As he worked, he explained that the idea of using cling film had come to him when he was making orthotics for a lady with severely ulcerated legs. As he wrapped my legs in the plaster soaked bandages, he explained that he had tried tubular bandages on this poor lady, but her skin was breaking down, and so much gory fluids were seeping through the dressing. He noticed his package of sandwiches sitting on his desk, and it was then he had his brainwave. He carefully explained the whole process and spared no detail in his description. I would have preferred that the conversation had followed a different route, but I had to admire the technician's love of his work.

The plaster quickly set and just as quickly he used a plaster saw to cut off the cast to make moulds of my feet.

As I left, I looked at the sandwiches in the kiosk. Mayonnaise and tomato had seeped in between the baguettes and the cling film wrap. I decided that I didn't feel hungry.

A while later, the splints arrived. It only struck me then that they looked horrible. They looked like a medieval instrument of torture. I put them in my car and left them there. I left them for weeks and carried on life tripping and falling. In the same way that Nicolas Andry's colleagues shunned him, I ignored the derivative of his inventions.

After a particularly bad fall after my dropped foot caught itself on the carpet, I decided that I must try them. The straps rubbed until my leg bled and the instep dug in, but I suddenly felt more confident. Over the next few weeks, I sorted the chaffing and very quickly I wouldn't go out without them.

Sometime later, my left knee took the unilateral decision not to perform the function that it had done daily since I started to walk. When you are standing your knees are naturally locked straight, you don't have to think about it. I was standing by the sink, and it just buckled. By this time, I had fallen many times, but now I started falling backwards like a felled tree. This was quite unnerving and resulted in me smashing the back of my head against the tarmac. The same thing happened a few days later, when I was standing next to the car.

I spoke with Doc, who referred me to a local orthotics department for a knee brace. This was a private clinic and very smart. The technician looked young, very young. We chatted about his motorbike parked outside, a beautiful vintage Indian bike. Private orthotics is obviously a great business to get into.

He measured me, asked me to walk and provided me with a knee brace.

It worked. Perhaps after a few centuries, Nicolas can be forgiven.

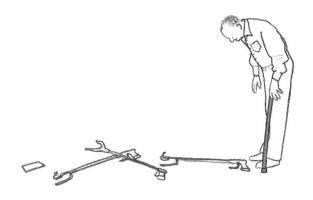

CHAPTER 9

LOSING MY GRIP

I am losing my grip. That is literally losing my grip. I'm not losing my grip on reality, that has always been quite loose. Now I am not able to pick many things up anymore.

I have mentioned that one of the first symptoms I noticed was that I could wobble the last digit of my forefinger in an extraordinary way. I could wave my hand, and it would look like it wasn't attached.

Not long after we ordered some new settees and so Diane and I decided to move the old one. We carried them out of the back door to take them down the side of the house. The lifting wasn't a problem, but it kept slipping out of my hands much to Diane's frustration.

It seems that loss of grip is a key diagnostic feature of the condition I have. It is the main clinical feature that distinguishes it from far more rapidly progressing Motor Neuron Disease. However frustrating it makes life I can still be glad that I have fingers that for many jobs are about as much use as a bunch of sausages.

I drop things. My walking sticks are continually falling to the floor. If cooking, knives, plates, pans and food go flying. Health and safety is an evident reason to take a lot of care and to stay out of the kitchen when I'm creating a culinary masterpiece. I am always reaching for grab sticks to pick something up. I have to have more than one grab stick. What else would I do if I dropped a grab stick?

As things progressed, my grip weakened, now my fingers sort of hang straight or bend backwards. Some things are more comfortable to hold than others. In the shower, soap and shower gel spend most of their time on the floor. Almost everything slips out of my fingers.

I hold a glass in much the same way as a sea lion. I was given a set of large handle cutlery to try, a bit like an oversized version of the cutlery babies use. As my fingers don't bend around the handle and I grip between my thumb and forefinger, I didn't find them any more straightforward to use than ordinary cutlery. As my fingers don't bend, picking cutlery up from a table is a problem, and I have to slide them to hang over the edge before I can hold them.

I never had beautiful handwriting, but what I had progressed from poor to illegible. I have always liked art and having more time allowed me to do more. I did a graphic design course and loved it. The more I did, the more I enjoyed painting and drawing. I like drawing detail which seems counter-intuitive and plays to my weaknesses; however, it works for me.

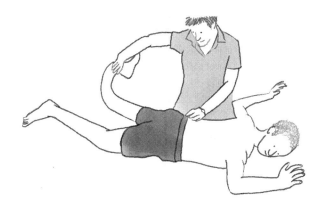

CHAPTER 10

PHYSIOTHERAPISTS

In 1859 Victoria Princess Royal and wife of Prince Frederick was in labour with her first child. Unfortunately, the birth didn't go well, and the baby's left arm was irreversibly damaged. As a child, the young Frederick grew up with a useless and withered arm. This was a great concern to his parents as he was destined to rule his country, and in those days, any deformity would be viewed as a weakness. Princess Victoria, therefore, recruited the help of the country's leading physiotherapists who devised a series of contraptions and routines to help restore strength in the arm.

Before he was one year old, he was given drastic electric shock therapy. Once a week, the arm was shoved inside the carcass of a freshly killed animal so that the heat might improve the shrivelled tissue. The young Prince's right arm was bound to his body so that his left arm would have to work. At the age of four, he was placed in a body-stretching machine a bit like a medieval rack, a contraption that wouldn't be out of place in a torture chamber. After some years, it became apparent that the treatment wasn't working and was discontinued. The main impact of the treatment on the prince was severe emotional trauma, probably shaping his future life and decisions. The prince went on to be Keiser Wilhelm II of Germany who catastrophically lead his country into the First World War.

Physiotherapy has come on a long way since those days, and I am not aware that it has had a role in the initiation of other major world conflicts around. I know several physiotherapists and they are all kind, warm and friendly people. However, like doctors, they have a detached view of pain. Believe me, this is a good thing if your life is on the line you want a doctor that will do everything necessary to save you and is not distracted by your screams. Generally, doctors aim to reduce suffering, physiotherapists, on the other hand, strive for pain, it is a necessary part of exercising and building your muscles.

There are a few things that you should know about how to respond to a physiotherapist. If they ask you 'are you OK?' never say 'Yes, I'm fine.' That is the wrong answer, and the inevitable response will be "Well, we'll ramp things up a bit then.", if you are OK then you are not working hard enough, and they will immediately increase the resistance. Good physiotherapists have a cache of similar questions to catch you out. 'Is that weight too heavy?' 'Is that uncomfortable?' or 'Are you on your last legs?'

My first experience of physiotherapists was a muscle assessment. On the instruction of the therapist, I pushed and pulled against the resistance of their hold. Each activity was designed to test a specific muscle and marked on a scale of 1 to 5. 1 is just a flicker of movement, 5 being able to move the full range against strong resistance. At my last assessment some time ago, many of my muscles were 4, they could move against some resistance, others were 3 they could counter the effects of gravity, a few were 2, and couldn't move against the force of gravity. My left wrist falls into this category, and if I lift my arm, my hand hangs down. The worst effect of this is if I try and wave at someone with this hand. As I lift my arm to vertical, my hand moves from it hanging position and flips over backwards, awkwardly reminiscent of a camp Nazi salute.

I regularly go for hydrotherapy, and I love it. The warm water soothes aching muscles, and without the hindrance of gravity, I can accomplish exercises that otherwise, I would find impossible, and without the fear of falling. As I share the pool with other regulars as well as people who can only make it irregularly, some use the ramp to walk in, others use a hoist, but most like me use a chair that fixes to a crane that lifts up the chair, is swung out and lowered into the water. This is operated by a hand crank giving the physiotherapists an opportunity for a bit of exercise.

I get on with my sequence of exercises. It includes walking across the pool forwards, backwards and sideways. I then hold onto the rail at the side, and with an armband placed over my foot, I lift my right leg up and down and side to side before transferring to the other foot. The others have their own exercises designed to address their specific condition, some using floats, others working directly with the physiotherapist. There are times when a line of ageing men line up on the pool rail looking like some hideous ballet class practising their Dégagé and Plié.

CHAPTER 11

STAIRLIFT TO HEAVEN

At the end of his life, the overfed Henry VIII weight had ballooned to nearly 30 stone. Perhaps he took rather too much to comfort eating after chopping the head off a tiresome wife or a troublesome advisor. He also suffered from painful festering ulcers on his legs and had trouble standing and walking. He was living at Whitehall Palace, presumably big enough that he could live comfortably on one level. However, there was a 20ft staircase to go outside. John Foxe, a contemporary historian, described an engine that was used to lower the corpulent Henry down the stairs when he wanted to walk in his garden. The contraption probably used a block and tackle and a small army of unlucky servants, fearful of letting go, to winch a throne up and down.

In the 1920's Mr Crispin wanted to help a sick friend get up and down the stairs and developed a stairlift. He called it the inclinator and started the Inclinator Company of America. The design consisted of a folding chair and footrest which moved up and down a track fastened to the stairs. It has hardly changed over the subsequent years and is more or less in keeping with what we see today.

When I was younger, I worked in a building with five flights of stairs. I would run up them, two steps at a time without a thought. I went up and down them many times each day. I knew them so well that I could surf down them, skimming off the outer edge of each step, with my hands gliding down the handrail so I could get down in ultra-quick time. I didn't think about it, just seemed instinctive, although I wouldn't have done this in front of my boss.

As the years passed, I grew up a little and took a bit more time climbing the stairs. The need to charge around lessened. I might phone rather than go upstairs to ask a simple question, and usually, there was a younger staff member about to answer the door. I would still go up and down the stairs many times each day.

Before work one day, I took my daughter to her nursery. As I climbed the stairs with Emily in my arms, I stopped to rest on the middle step. It wasn't long before I stopped even when I wasn't carrying Emily. Gradually climbing the stairs got harder and harder. By the time I went to see the GP, I had started climbing on all fours, but I could still get up and down well enough.

Over a few years, it gradually became harder as well as less safe. Going up or down a step wasn't a controlled action. There came a time when I realised that each time I used the stairs, I was at risk of falling. Obviously, in a house that is a problem. Making a bedroom downstairs wasn't a practical option without making too many sacrifices. So we had to look for alternatives.

We could move to a bungalow. The word bungalow derives from the Hindi word Bangala, used to describe a house in the Bengali style and popular amongst officials in colonial India. It does not originate, as my friend's dad told me when I was young and so believed for many years, from builders who have run out of bricks and decide to "Bung a low roof on". If you can't climb stairs, a bungalow would seem like a sensible option. That is if you can get one. Most builders aren't building them anymore, they are not the most efficient way to make money from building land. The proportion of new build houses that are bungalows has gone down year on year and is now less than 1%. Of course, there is already a stock of single floor homes, but that is insufficient for demand. Many people find bungalows convenient, not just those with disabilities and the elderly, so there is a lot of competition. Apparently, Aberdeen has the fewest bungalows of any city in the UK, so bad luck if you live there. As I look now on Rightmove, there are just four Bungalows for sale in, and around the city. If you have mobility problems, you are unlikely to be the first in the queue. None of these though are accessible without some alteration, so you might have to send someone else out to view them. In fact, there are lots of old bungalows that are really inaccessible. They may have corridors that are too narrow for a wheelchair, a bathroom that is too small to get into and steps up or down to the front door, sometimes lots of steps. Not much point for someone who is infirm to move to a bungalow if you have to climb 30 steps to get in.

The shortage of suitable housing is more extensive than just bungalows. Habinteg did some research in 2010 found that 84% of homes in England do not allow someone using a wheelchair to get to and through the front door without difficulty. The number of homes that a wheelchair user could just move into is less than 0.5%. If you look at the number of wheelchair users in the UK (over 600,000), there are about 80,000 people that are not living in suitable housing.

We like our house, our children need their space, and we didn't want to move to something less than we have at the moment. When we looked, we realised that our options were limited. There weren't a lot of bungalows available in our area, well not in the right price bracket, the right size or location. It isn't a big town so we drove around and found only four that we thought would meet our needs. None of these were for sale.

We would need another answer. In the paper, I read an advert "Free booklet, everything you need to know about stairlifts." Brilliant, just what I need. I knew nothing about stairlifts. I had never tried one and couldn't think that I had ever seen one other than on TV adverts. I went to their website, completed the online form and pressed send.

Two minutes passed, then the phone rang. "Hello Mr McVey, I am in your area tomorrow, would you be free to talk about your need for a stairlift."

He had taken me by surprise "My you are quick off the mark, actually I'm not ready to buy one yet, I was just looking for some information first."

"Yes, exactly Mr McVey, I understand. Would you be about at 2pm and I could show you everything you need to know about our stairlifts." I realised at this point that he was quite pushy, so I lied

"I'm not available tomorrow",

"So I can make it next week."

"I would rather wait until I have had time to read to the booklet" I responded

"It will have arrived by tomorrow, so what time on Monday would be best with you" At this point I started to wonder how to end this call.

"I don't want a visit, I just want to look at the information."

"Quite right, Mr McVey, I wouldn't want to see other manufacturers if I were you, there are some high-pressure sales in this business. We are not like that, our product sells itself, so we don't use pressure sales, We are the best in the industry. So what time on Monday did we say?" Ahhhhhhh

"NO I'm not about on Monday, and I don't..."

"I thought you said you were, well any day next week."

"I don't want to see you at all, I'm not about any day next week. I just wanted some information about stairlifts."

"Why didn't you say Mr McVey, there is no need to be angry. I'm only here to help. Can I send you a catalogue?"

"Yes, that would be fine, thanks."

"No worries, I've got your address on our system. Rather than post it, I'll drop it by, which day are you in next week."

I realise that rudeness is the only option. "If you can't post it, forget it. I need to go Bye."

As I put the phone down I can hear "So can I call you next...BRRRR"

I breathe a sigh. At least that is over. I was wrong, and the fun had only just started. The phone rang, oh no, not again. I answered, and it was a different voice, phew.

"Mr McVey, I understand you would like information about our award-winning stairlifts, I happen to be in your area tomorrow..."

I realised sales staff deemed beyond the pale for timeshare sales have a refuge in stairlift sales. I wonder if this one has won the national stairlift salesman of the year award, perhaps with special recognition for selling most new stairlifts together with twenty-year maintenance contract to bungalow owners

The calls continued but were now responded to with an abrupt. "I have no need for a stairlift. Goodbye". Even this didn't deter one relentless salesman, and I had to cut him off three times.

I never did get the booklet, so I did some research online and ordered a few brochures.

As well as the conventional stairlift, it is now possible to put a small elevator in the house. It was an expensive option but seemed worth the consideration. As the lift rises, it raises a hatch that covers the hole in the floor. Obviously, the positioning of this is essential, if you don't want to lift unsuspecting visitors and squidge them between the top of the lift and the ceiling. In our house there aren't too many significant areas downstairs that have no use, while the lift is perhaps a meter square, you also have to have space to manoeuvre into it. The problem is compounded upstairs. The ideal location downstairs would bring the lift up in the bathroom. The sound of the lift doors closing would strike fear into anyone using the toilet or taking a bath. Having thought through the options, we decided that an elevator lift was impractical for our house.

Having ruled out elevators, we returned to looking at stairlifts. On Google I found endless adverts for stairlift companies, however, after a time, I realised that there were only a few manufacturers.

Most manufacturers appear to assume that the only colour you will ever want for your stairlift is a hospital beige. The beautiful mobile looking young woman on the advert seems pleased with the choice of colour.

I discovered that there are straight lifts and more expensive ones for curved staircases. Manufacturers have obviously invested a little more in making the curved ones look stylish, and they are priced accordingly. The brochures appear to make the assumption that if you have a curve in your staircase, you must live in a grander house. Our stairs are dead straight, so we chose from the cheaper ranges.

At the bottom of our stairs; however, there is no wall, so apparently, we needed a means to move the track out of the way so that it isn't a trip hazard. There are two ways to do this, one is to lift the end of the rail so that instead of tripping over it, you are likely to poke your eye out. The other method involved a moving track that extended beyond the bottom step when needed.

The moving track was a more elegant solution and only made by one manufacturer. Unfortunately, this ruled out the one company that offered a range of fabric covers.

I called and made an appointment for Bob to come and visit. Bob is a good, trustworthy and reliable name so I had high hopes that he would sort me out.

Two days later Bob arrived as arranged. Bob was a short man wearing a smart but obviously well-worn suit. I warmed quickly to Bob as he told me that he had worked with the same company for 25 years and that despite its growth, it was still a caring family company. I felt confident in Bob's dependable hands. The week before Bob had installed a lift for his elderly and infirm mother and it had already changed her life. It did seem a bit coincidental that after 25 years, this personal insight occurred just days before coming to see me.

Bob asked me what I wanted from a stairlift. I wasn't quite sure how to answer that question, was it a trick question.

"Actually Bob, I was hoping for something that would transport me from downstairs to upstairs, oh and vice versa." I was pleased with myself for specifying vice versa.

"I see" replied Bob as if I had given him a useful insight into my particular needs. "I'll just measure up your stairs to see what will work for you." There are not lots of options, so I was a little surprised that after 25 years he wasn't able to do this as he glanced at the stairs on his way in, but I was reassured by his thoroughness. He got his tape measure out and went off to measure the staircase. He came back with a diagram and a list of measurements. "I just need to measure you now." He measured the length of my thighbone and my sitting height, and in my mind, I could justify both measurements. He then measured my waist. "What's that for?" I asked. Apparently, it was for an automatic seatbelt. This really got me thinking, why did he need my waist measurement for an automatic belt, he surely doesn't believe that my stomach might exceed the maximum setting.

Bob got out his calculator and tapped in some numbers, writing the results down before banging in some more numbers. Bob looked concerned, he sucked the end of his pen, made a clicking sound with his tongue and sighed.

"Is there a problem?"

Bob didn't look up from his paper, and he was concentrating too hard to respond immediately. After a short while, he said: "It's OK we can do it."

I asked what the problem was.

"I didn't think that it would fit in the space" I was surprised by this as our stairs are about as standard as you can get, I suspect that the builders did nothing more than buy and install a standard staircase kit.

Bob clarified the situation for me. "It's your thigh bones, they are unusually long, but it does fit in."

"If they didn't fit," Bob was reassuring, "there would be two options, the first would be to cut into the bannister. The other would be…" He didn't finish the sentence but made a chopping action over his knees. Things had taken a surprisingly sinister turn.

"There is one type of lift that will work for you" And with that Bob went on to describe the options. I opted for an automatic footrest and moving rail. "And of course the seatbelt is standard," I asked why there was a seatbelt, is the ride high-speed and bumpy? I have never fallen off a chair while sitting. Bob knowingly told me that frail people do fall off their chairs, besides it has to be fitted by law. I have never been much of a rebel, but I decided that perhaps when people are not looking, I will live dangerously and not fasten it.

"Is it quiet?" I asked I didn't want to wake my daughter every time I went to bed. Bob reassuringly said, "The lift itself is quite quiet, the lift wouldn't wake you up."

"You can choose whatever cover you like for the seat so that it matches your home decor". said Bob Wow this was news to me I thought I was limited to the six bright colours in the catalogue in addition to beige. Bob clarified that it was any colour out of that selection of six colours. Unfortunately, when we decorated our hall, we had a choice of hundreds of colours and limitless design options. Life would have been a lot simpler if there were only six options. Each colour would stand out like a sore thumb. I pointed this out to Bob who explained that is why they do the particular shade of beige colour, cleverly designed to clash with any colour equally. Diane and I had decided that the blue colour was the least offensive and we could decorate around it.

"You will be pleased to know Mr McVey, the seat is made from a wipe-clean plastic" I pointed out that I'm not incontinent. "Well just as well to be prepared in case." I may never become incontinent, but I wonder whether I should get ready for that day and cover my chair, car seat and bed with plastic sheeting.

Bob said that it could be installed quickly and I signed to buy. True to his word, two weeks later, the installers arrived. Within a couple of hours, they had fixed the track, decided it was the wrong one, uninstalled it and left. A few days later, they returned, and within a few hours, I was the owner of a smart new stairlift. As Bob had said, the lift itself wasn't noisy, apart from the added beeping sound. As the chair climbed beep, beep, beep and as it descended beep, beep, beep. I asked the installer to switch the b*@% beep off, I begged and offered bribes but to no avail. "Sorry mate, I can't switch the beeping off, it's the law" I felt that I was remiss not being genned up on stairlift law. Apparently moving mechanical things need to beep, so I decided with my new rebel status I will try and muffle the sound.

Daniel and Emily had to try the lift first. Fortunately, it didn't have the attraction of a ride at Alton Towers and they quickly tired of it. That evening getting to bed was a pleasure, when I finally managed to get a go.

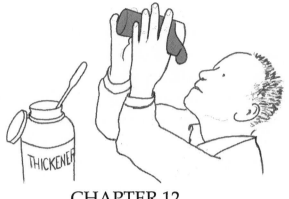

CHAPTER 12

SWALLOWING

On a visit to the Peak District, it struck me how much the British love picnics. A couple seated on two large padded folding chairs either side of a picnic table laid out with a gingham table cloth and Tupperware boxes, found the majestic hills and picturesque valleys to be a less enticing picnic spot than some dingy layby complete with overflowing bins and a long-abandoned burned-out car. This isn't a criticism, it's an observation, and we are the same. We love going on picnics. The anticipation of a picnic is filled with mental images of lying on rugs in remote luxuriant fields, under the shade of an oak tree. The reality was sitting in the car, looking out over a spectacular view or instead it would have been if there was any visibility through the drizzly wet fog. For all we could see, we might as well been in a Wolverhampton car park. As children,

Daniel and Emily loved picnics so much that on wet days we would set up a picnic in the lounge.

This time the rolls were unusually tricky to eat. When I chewed and swallowed, it just seemed to stay in my throat. Not that distressing feeling when you feel a gulp of food going into your windpipe, and your reflexes take control in the belief it could be your last breath. It was just stuck and however much swallowing I did it wouldn't go down. I tried drinking water with no effect on the bread, and now my mouth was full of water. Eventually, I had to cough, and while this sorted the problem I spluttering water everywhere.

I already knew that swallowing may be an issue that I would encounter, Doc had explained the probability, it was mentioned in all the literature, and it was a frequent topic of discussion in online groups. Doc referred me for some swallowing tests, and soon afterwards, I was given an appointment at a clinic at the local hospital.

A nurse directed me to put on a gown, and I was soon taken into the X-ray room. They sat me on the radiography table and set up the camera. I was given a glass of water, a particularly unpleasant peach yoghurt and pot of barium to drink while the radiologist and a speech therapist studied X-ray images of my swallowing.

Afterwards, I met with a speech therapist. She described the structure of my throat and explained where my swallowing mechanism was getting things wrong. At that time, I just needed some advice.

This was the start of having problems with swallowing. Some foods are worse than others. Unfortunately, bread and chips seem to be the worst. Much later after a particularly bad patch, I saw another speech therapist. I was having difficulty swallowing water. It sounds mad, but water is actually quite challenging to gulp down. Thicker liquids such as soups are much more manageable. The therapist prescribed me a thickening agent to make drinks more gloopy. The thickening agent can be used in any beverage or soup. I could stir a few spoons into my beer at the pub to give it the consistency of wallpaper paste. The therapist said that there were two thickener options. One type is made from guar gum, the miracle ingredient of 1980's scam diet pills and revealed as having no basis in evidence by "That's Life". Apparently, although of no use for dieting, it does thicken liquids well. Unfortunately, it also has quite a noticeable taste. The second thickener option was starch-based which is claimed to have little flavour and so this option was recommended by the therapist. When my prescription arrived, there were three massive tins. I couldn't imagine taking a tin with me to a restaurant, and I have certainly never seen other diners with a large thickener tin on their table. Perhaps they discretely decant some of the powder into smaller containers. At the moment, I am fortunate as my dysphasia comes and goes. My swallowing was improving, and I was less often spluttering over a glass of water.

When I next spoke with Doc, I mentioned that I had been prescribed the thickener. He asked if I had used it. I sheepishly admitted that it is all still in its tins.

"That's funny," he responded, "I haven't met a patient yet who has used the stuff."

There are still times when I have to take extra care in my choice of food because it isn't very dignified or pleasant for my companions when their meal is interrupted with me spluttering and coughing back my chips or beer, but I have yet to try the thickener. In the future, it will get worse, and I may get frequent aspiration pneumonia or not be able to eat enough food. At this time, I can be fitted with a feeding peg. This upgrade is a tube put through my abdomen into my stomach and equipped with a handy closure cap. Instead of going to the trouble of drinking beer or eating crisps and chocolate, it can all be liquidised and the delicious concoction gravity fed through the tube, directly into my stomach. More probably I would be fed a sterile, nutritionally complete, unpleasant-smelling grey gloop. For the moment I am content with imbibing my treats the old fashioned way.

CHAPTER 13

OCCUPATIONAL THERAPISTS

It has always struck me that speech therapist is an odd name for someone who helps with swallowing. At some point, a GP must have puzzled about where to refer perpetually choking patient and decided to send them to a speech therapist on the basis that they know something about the relevant problematic bits.

Occupational therapist is another health job whose title seems like a bit of a misnomer. If you ask people about their occupation, they will tell you about their work, unless they are Nazi's who might think you were talking about Poland. They are very unlikely to tell you about how they chop up their food or wipe their bum. The other context you use the term occupation is concerning toilets, but it seems a bit excessive to seek a therapist when you find the bathroom is occupied.

The National Society for the Promotion of Occupational Therapy was founded in the US in 1917 by William Rush Dunton, amongst others. He considered titles such as "work-cure", "ergo therapy"(ergo being Greek for "work"), and "creative occupations" but decided that these were no better so stuck with occupational therapy even though he didn't think that it accurately described what they did.

Industrial accidents, tuberculosis, World War I, meant that there was no shortage of disabled people at the beginning of the 20th Century. Until this time work therapy had been associated with mental illness. The escalating number of wounded soldiers led the US military to train occupational therapists to help with their rehabilitation. They used activities such as crafts, but also looked at how to assist daily living. Until this time medicine rarely considered individuals social, economic or practical day to day needs. Their success was soon followed in the UK.

You can still see the results of Duton's treatment. Thirteen years after his death, his collection of quilts made by his patients during their therapy led to him being inducted into the Quilter's Hall of Fame.

When you need some help at home, an occupational therapist is probably the person you will see. On my first visit from an occupational therapist, she watched me get out of chairs, get on and off the bed and on and off the toilet. These are things that you don't often do in front of someone you have just met.

A few days later, a delivery arrived of tools and gadgets that might help. A raised toilet seat and a toilet frame, a bar to help getting out of bed and raisers to heighten my chair. She had also included a sock aid, although she had explained that some people find it difficult to use. It appears that I am in that category, it seemed to be no help and was physically more demanding than wrestling with my socks. The Occupational Therapist did suggest I bought some diabetic socks as these don't have an elastic band and are easy to put on and happily these worked a treat.

On occasions, the Occupational Therapist has found me all sorts of equipment from transfer boards to walking frames. We tried some things like a rising chair which although it worked well wasn't practical in our home. I wanted a lifting device to get me off the floor after a fall, and I knew people who had used a contraption called a Camel. The Camel was invented by David Garman who was trying to solve the problem of helping a relative get in and out of the bath. He used a stack of inflatable lifting bags attached to a pump. As the bags inflated, the relative was gently lifted to a position where they could stand up. David realised that the same idea could be used to lift people who had fallen on the floor.

My first enquiries to get one was met with the instruction to call an ambulance if I couldn't get off the floor. This is probably a sensible precaution as I wouldn't necessarily know how much damage I had done to myself. It would be reasonable if there weren't days or weeks when I have fallen numerous times. I would effectively appropriate an ambulance for my personal use which didn't seem a practical or cost-effective option. Besides most times, it is reasonably apparent that my injuries are minor. The day after this advice I fell in the drive and had to call an Ambulance. As with all emergency ambulances, they had lifting equipment, a smaller version of the Camel called an Elk, but they were remarkably strong, so quickly and deftly lifted me using a towel onto my wheelchair. I wrote a grumpy letter to the occupational therapists pointing out the lack of wisdom and limitations in their advice and was helped by a letter of support from Doc.

Sometimes you have to be a bit obstinate, and my grumbling seemed to do the job. A few days later, I had a call from another occupational therapist. She arranged to come out to discuss the options with me. Generally lodging a complaint isn't the best way to get on with people who are going to help you. I thought it best to bring this up with her first. Happily, it was soon apparent that she was on my side.

She agreed that I needed a Camel, but as with so many things these days the purse strings were held in some distant office by someone with a close eye on the balance sheet but no understanding of needs. She would, therefore, be forced to show why less expensive options wouldn't work. The first option would be to supply a hoist. These are large metal frames moved on coasters, and although expensive they always have a supply of these personal cranes in store. In due course, one arrived for us to test.

Being an awkward sort of person, I don't fall in the same place. One hoist would be needed upstairs, and another downstairs, neither would help if I fell outside or in parts of the house where the equipment wouldn't fit. So, at last, the distant office agreed to fund a Camel. It soon arrived, and we spent an hour practising connecting the tubes and lifting me up and down off the lounge floor. There are a few things to learn to operate it safely, so Diane, Emily and Daniel all had instructions. It is well designed, and although there are several tube connections and buttons to press, it is intuitive and straightforward to use.

A few weeks later, I fell again on the drive. Diane fetched the Camel and unrolled it. It was a chance to test it in action. The machine comprises a stack of airbags. Each is fitted with an easy to connect tube which links into a pump. Diane efficiently set it up, ready for me to crawl onto the uninflated stack. Diane would then press the buttons to inflate the bags and lift me from the floor to a seated position where I can transfer onto a wheelchair.

While Diane was setting it up, I realised that the drive was quite damp and this was making me cold. Fortunately, Diane had also brought out the slide sheet, an accessory that had been brought with the Camel. The slide sheet is simply a nylon sheet, so we saw no need to practice using it. I took the sheet out of the bag and laid it out next to me. I then rolled onto the sheet. I immediately discovered a crucial property of a slide sheet. Perhaps the name should have given it away, but a slide sheet is actually a large sleeve. The two layers of nylon enable a carer to push someone on a surface. It effectively reduces the friction to less than a banana skin on an ice rink. What I hadn't reckoned on was that our drive is on a bit of a slope. The slide sheet did its real job well, too well, so gravity took hold, propelling me toboggan like down the drive.

Some gadgets and adaptations work for some people but not others, everyone is different, so there is always a bit of trial and error. I have had many useful suggestions and some less so. One occupational therapist suggested buying a spaghetti fork out of one of these magazines. A small electric motor spun the fork head to wind on the spaghetti. As we don't often eat spaghetti, it seemed a bit too specialist.

The internet has many examples of creative people with my condition who have discovered their inner inventor. They have adapted and repurposed everyday items to let them continue their lives as before. Every one of us has found some adaptions, sometimes very simple. I discovered that a butter knife and wooden spoon are the ideal tools to open ring pull cans. The blade lifts the ring so the spoon handle can fit through it and with the ball of the spoon resting on the can the handle acts as a useful lever. Others have been much more creative. One man designed and had trousers made with a high back and Velcro fastenings to be comfortable in a wheelchair. Another fastened a belt to the back of his chair, this went over his shoulder and clipped onto a wristband. When he leant forward the belt would lift his hand towards his mouth so he could feed himself. Yet another made a mechanism cut out of a plastic bottle. The device consisted of overlapping hinged plates that fitted armadillo fashion over the fingers. Fishing lines were threaded through each finger and attached to a band on the upper arm.

As he bent his arm, the contraption curled bending the fingers to grip something.

I have also invented a tool to turn on a plug socket, apparatus to reach things that have fallen under the settee and a device to help me find my sleeve when putting on a coat. Actually, Diane has pointed out that these are all sticks, and I cannot really claim to have invented the stick since their use predates the evolution of humans.

Some shops sell gadgets that can help will all sorts of jobs. We get one posted through our door once a month. I can never work out the economics of these catalogue companies as we only bought one thing from them, a hot water dispenser that we thought maybe safer for me than a kettle. We quickly discovered that contrary to the advertised promises, the design made it more likely we would end up spraying scalding water over our hands, and so we sent it back. We received a full refund so on the credit side they hadn't made any money from us, on the debit side, they have sent us tens of catalogues, each one of must-have cost a few pounds in postage, printing and administration.

I have pawed through these catalogues with the same feelings of desire I felt as a youngster looking at the tents in the Blacks camping catalogue. I would wonder if the automatic can opener would only open one can before giving up, if I needed a long-handled brush for my balding head or a sponge on a stick to reach parts that don't see the light of day. I hope that I am a little time off needing absorbent pants, but even these interested me.

Some catalogues combine health and mobility products with other solutions that they claim will improve your everyday life. They have some odd things, a recent brochure included a chain to hold your napkin round your neck, video camera sunglasses whose suggested uses seem to verge on the illegal and a machine that looks like it was invented by a bored and overly inquisitive milkman which claims to enrich your love life.

The gadget that I have looked for and would buy without hesitation is something that comfortably keeps my trousers up. My body is changing shape. When I was in my 20s my Mr Man body shape was Mr Skinny, now it is more like Mr Bump. A round body with skinny legs and arms, frequently covered with a bandage. One difficulty with this body shape is underpants. For most people, their bum has the little appreciated function of providing a projection to hang underpants and trousers from. A small elastic or a belt and you are sorted. My gluteus maximus (now minimus) has the opposite effect, so my underpants and trousers now have nothing to hang on to. A bit like trying to put an elastic band over a slippery cone. As I walked, I would feel everything starting to slip. Walking with two sticks also means that there is no free hand. Nothing to hitch things up. Fortunately for everyone, due to sturdy elastic belts, I was able to maintain most of my dignity. Underpants were a different matter, and as I walked around, they would catapult uncomfortably down my legs, so I was effectively going commando, and still with the risk of much, much worse. It took several experiments to find pants that would hold.

Some of the tools are designed to help with packaging. Packaging designers are almost universally idiots.

I have had years of experience in unpackaging toys my children have received at Christmas. When I was young toys came in a box. You opened it and tipped out all the parts. Occasionally there was a cellophane window or some cardboard partitions. Nowadays, toys are displayed to look spectacular in their box, but unpacking them is no job for a child. Once you are past the cardboard container and the moulded plastic cover, you find that the hundred little pieces are individually attached to a backing board by wires. These are mechanically twisted and tied with the addition of plastic spacers and screws. After an hour of painfully untwisting wires, you are rewarded with a bored child looking at the tiny pile of plastic crap next to a mountain of unrecyclable rubbish and deciding that it more fun could be had by sticking their head in the box.

The purpose of food packaging is to keep nasty bugs out, be tamper-proof, make it easy to stack, look attractive, as well as display some useful and marketing information. It seems these days this requires numerous layers of cardboard and plastic, theoretically designed to peel apart. Ham slices are packed in a plastic tray with a thinner plastic lid. Yoghurt is packed in a plastic tub with a foil lid and another plastic lid. The designers helpfully add tiny little tabs. Having difficulties with my grip, these are universally too small to hold. I have tried using barbeque tongs, forceps and even my teeth to attempt to wrestle these open. The inevitable outcome is that the tab tears off and the packaging has been mauled so badly that the only solution is to attack it with a sharp kitchen knife. I bought some heavy-duty scissors to get into the packaging. Unfortunately, these were helpfully sealed into a heavy plastic pack that would withstand a nuclear apocalypse.

The design of jar lids has changed, so they have a sloping rather than straight edge, making them harder to grip and therefore much harder to open. Ring pulls on tins are of no help if you are not able to lift them or pull them off.

There are various devices that you can buy to help. I have tried most of them, and many are next to useless. Occasionally though I discover something that really helps. I have a tool that fits over screw bottle tops and gives enough leverage to open bottles of fizzy drinks. I have also found a device that releases the vacuum in jars, making them easy to open. It can be difficult to find genuinely useful implements amongst rotating spaghetti forks and banana slicers. I end up finding a way to do things out of necessity. I have not found a tool to help with ring pulls that beats a butter knife and a wooden spoon. Perhaps I should package these up and sell them to Kleeneze.

CHAPTER 14

CARS

Schoolboys dream of fast cars. In a schoolboy's mind during the 1960s and 70s, the AC Cobra was one of the coolest cars on the planet. It was a beautiful, open-topped roadster, and it was very swift. Such would be the draw to the opposite sex that simply parking would draw sexy bikini-clad woman to inexplicably jump into the passenger seat.

Unfortunately for schoolboys, they grow up, and life turns out to be a little different. A few with the support of a loving wife, have a family and their business becomes very successful. They remember their dream and decide to exchange their boring new BMW for a gorgeous, curvaceous old AC Cobra. An original may cost hundreds of thousands of pounds, which is great because now everyone knows how successful they are.

To maintain balance in the world, it becomes essential for them to jettison the exhausted and weary old wife for a new model, flawless in looks but preferably none too bright. Now balance and harmony has returned to the world, tiresome new replaced with beautiful old, counterbalanced by knackered old replaced by beautiful new. The natural order has returned, and now all is happy and harmonious in the world, or rather it would be if it wasn't for that annoying alimony case. Doesn't his new ex-wife realise how all these little essentials take up so much money? She should curb her frivolously wants to spend money on buying the children shoes, as if she hasn't heard of cobblers.

What happens if your career hasn't brought you such wealth and fortune, and you still have this dream. Well, don't worry you can get the authentic AC experience. For just a few hundred pounds, you could pick up an AC Invacar.

You might assume that this is shortened from Invaluable Car. Whatever colour you would like, unless it's blue forget it, they only come in blue. After you have been kicked out by your exasperated wife, don't worry, you have no need to find a nubile replacement. While this has the same Babe Magnet effect as the Cobra, it is set to repel rather than attract, and AC thoughtfully made the Invacar single-seater.

This is lucky as your once athletic body has long since gone to seed, and piles, halitosis and various unpleasant personal habits don't make for a high response rate on dating websites. Don't even try squeezing someone in, an ominous sign on the dashboard states "Passenger Carrying is Forbidden".

If you haven't seen an Invacar, picture a Robin Reliant, a three-wheeled car that for many years was the butt of many jokes and the perfect comic car for Del Boy Trotter in Only Fools and Horses. Now take the Reliant in its limited range of colours and paint it blue. Make it much smaller and uglier and just generally more crap and you pretty much have the glorious AC Invacar.

The Model 70 Invacar was initially designed by AC under contract from the Ministry of Health in the late 1960s, following previous invalid carriages. Many were built under contract by another company called Thundersley. To ensure that people with disabilities could blend inconspicuously into the community, the Ministry decided to make them all an unattractive shade of blue called Ministry Blue. The car was banned from motorway driving but reportedly could reach a top speed of 82 mph. As there were no public roads where legally you could open the throttle to achieve the full potential power of this machine I imagine that somewhere and at some time one must have been involved in a terrifying high-speed police chase. All Invacars were recalled and scrapped in 2000 when someone realised that as well as being hair raisingly scary they were also quite unsafe. By then, people had understood that it was much safer and in all ways better, to add a few simple levers to adapt a standard car. Despite all their shortcomings, I suspect that many owners loved their Invacars and the independence they gave.

I realised that something would need to adapt if I was to keep driving when I pulled up to the traffic lights near home.

I stopped and pulled on my handbrake. After a brief wait, the lights turned green. I, however, wasn't moving. I simply couldn't press the button to release the handbrake. Within seconds people behind were eagerly pointing out with their horns that I wasn't moving, presumably assuming that I simply hadn't noticed the green light. I put on my hazard lights and cars started pulling round now irate that I had temporarily blocked their way. The lights turned back to red, and by now those behind were developing a lifelong grudge as my immobility might delay their journey.

I was still struggling to release the button. My thumb simply didn't have the power. I tried with my other hand with no more luck. I was surprised that it was fastened so firmly, so I attempted a well-aimed karate chop.   I've seen experts cut through a stack of tiles, thus releasing a button shouldn't be a problem. The realisation that this was a mistake was immediate and painful.

In the cars behind me, voodoo dolls were being impaled with long pins, evil incantations chanted to bring curses on me, and future generations and shoots from the hedgerow were being fashioned into a wicker man.

I found my walking stick from the back seat and with it jammed it into the passenger footwell, and by pushing it against my mobile phone, which pressed against a firm wine gum and that in turn against the hand brake, acted as a lever enabling me to depress the button. This wasn't hands-free use of a mobile phone while driving, so I suppose that it was illegal and I doubt that at that point I would be able to explain the situation to a police officer without being taken into custody for being clearly in the middle of some strange mental health episode and for my own safety. Fortunately, the brake released and I was on my way again.

I realised that I had to get some help, so I arranged for a driving assessment, and a short while later I had an appointment at the local outreach centre. After an initial interview, I was taken for a drive in an adapted car. The car had an electric brake, and I could immediately see that this was now a necessity for me. It was also automatic, which meant that my weaker left leg had nothing to do. If I wanted to keep driving my next car would need to be automatic.

The car was also fitted with hand controls. Hand controls are mechanically simple, they are metal levers which enable you to operate the accelerator and brake by gripping a handle attached to the steering wheel. They are designed so that you can still use the pedals of the car if you prefer. I tried going around a housing estate using the hand controls. They are surprisingly intuitive and easy to operate, but for me, there was one difficulty they need good grip to use them, after ten minutes my arms were exhausted. Manual hand controls would not be for me, but the instructor gave me a catalogue of possible adaptions. Electronic hand controls are available as well as numerous adaptations that enable people with all types of severe impairments to drive confidently and safely. Apparently, it is entirely possible to drive a car with just one working limb.

Having decided to buy a new car, I started to research which model would suit me. I trawled through manufacturer's websites, sent for brochures and read reviews on specialist websites. I needed a car that was tall enough to get out of, had a large enough boot to fit a wheelchair, automatic and with an electric handbrake. Oh, yes, it had to be affordable.

I discovered that it was possible to retrofit an electric handbrake or add a mechanical lever that needs less effort to engage and release a manual handbrake, but neither seemed like an ideal option. Electric hand brakes were relatively new and certainly not the norm so gradually I was able to exclude most models until I was left with a shortlist of five or so cars. The shortlist included some that I couldn't find information about, so I went on a tour of showrooms to find out some more.

Three were unsuitable, one didn't have an automatic handbrake, another the seat was too near the ground, the boot was too small, and despite its hearse like looks, I wouldn't be seen dead in it. The last of the three had an automatic brake, but my floppy fingers just couldn't operate it.

The next I looked at was a Peugeot. I had had a second hand one before and as I drove home the speedometer packed in. I was suspicious that someone had tampered with the mileage and I had a big row with the garage, but in the end, I kept the car. I took a dislike to the car after that, but it just kept running without repairs so although unloved, it stuck with me for years. This Peugeot though looked ideal with some attractive features.

My preferred option was a Citroen. I had owned a Citroen before, and I loved it. The Citroen would have been perfect, but unfortunately, the production of the model I wanted had finished, and it would be sometime before the replacement was available. I was pleased to settle on the Peugeot

Once you have a car, you have to fill it with fuel. Petrol pumps are tricky beasts for me. The nozzle never faces in quite the right direction, and the hose only bends in directions that don't help. I can't depress the handle with one hand for long, so every few seconds change from one to another or grip with both. I did buy a device that was meant to help. It was merely a C shaped yellow plastic chip. The idea is that once you have depressed the handle, the clip holds it. That is the idea, in practice, I wasn't able to squeeze the handle quite enough to fit the clip. However much I struggled, it needed just a bit more strength. With two hands I could momentarily get there, but I needed a third hand to fit the clip. Eventually, I did manage to get the clip partly on, only for it to spring off and fly over the back of my car and into the middle of the forecourt. A man going to pay for his fuel saw the yellow object flash past him. He picked it up and looked up at the roof. Obviously confounded as to where this had come from. I tried to attract his attention, but the man had decided that the flying plastic object was just one of life's unsolvable mysteries, put it in the bin and carried on. I had decided that the gadget was pointless and by this time the tank was virtually full, so he had done me a favour.

Many disabled people will understand the frustration of filling a car with fuel. A few service stations are excellent and there are apps such as fuelService that help you arrange an arrival time with a service station so that someone can be on hand to help.

Many appear to make no effort to offer assistance. This is frustrating but is understandable for small independent stations where the one teenage staff member's first responsibilities are to lock themselves inside a glass-walled booth with the till so that it doesn't get nicked. It's hard to understand why major petrol retailers get it so wrong.

One of the dumbest initiatives of all time was the Northern Irish Renewable Heat Incentives Scheme. Under the scheme, millions of pounds were paid out to heat empty barns and deserted factories making a few entrepreneurial fraudsters very rich. Many petrol stations, including those of significant petrol retailers, use a system that I suspect was devised by the same person. They display a tiny little wheelchair sign and the words "Sound your horn for assistance."

As a driver, I know that there is something about a car horn that immediately raises my hackles. If I am driving in traffic when someone blasts their horn, I have no idea which car it was or even which direction the sound came. Have I cut in front of the blue mini behind? Perhaps it was the taxi next to me aggrieved that the van in front had decided to turn right resulting in a 20-second hold-up. Maybe a child had stepped out in front of the lorry ahead. Every car in the queue feels that they were on the receiving end of a shocking and unwarranted rebuke. Even when it becomes clear that it was the two young lads in the 1990s Fiesta retrofitted with a remarkable oversized large spoiler attracting the attention of their spotty mate on the pavement, my feeling of inner calm has been replaced by sizzling tension.

After sounding my horn, I have been asked: "What's up with you, mate!" The tone and manner of delivery made it unquestionably clear if my horn sounded again their concern for my welfare would become very real.

For these reasons sitting in a petrol forecourt sounding my horn isn't an attractive proposition. If it resulted in an attendant coming to assist, it is an embarrassment that I could live with. In 2014 Rica, a UK disability consumer research charity, sent disabled drivers to try filling their car at petrol stations. It appears that most had a miserable time, some waited and waited for help while attendants carried on oblivious to them. Others never got served at all.

If these stations wanted to do something helpful and straightforward perhaps they could kindly display a "No Disabled People" sign so that I could go to a station that can help.

CHAPTER 15

BUCKETGATE

The incident that my son Daniel refers to as "Bucketgate" started with my innocuous offer to clean the conservatory windows. We were getting ready for the family to come round for Easter. "Are you sure you can do that?" asks Diane, but I knew that she is too busy to make a fuss. "I can clean windows, no problem" I replied. Diane gets a bit protective which is both endearing and extremely frustrating. Ok, to be fair, there were times when she was right, like the time I couldn't climb some steps into a restaurant, so we went somewhere else, but there were also times when she was wrong, and I was fine. I would crow that I hadn't fallen, but Diane retorted that I had got away with it.

A few minutes earlier carpet fitters had arrived to lay a new carpet in our hall. It would be a good idea to keep out of their way for a while. Anyway, it was just splashing some water over a few windows so what could go wrong. I had a sponge and squeegee on a stick, so as long as I didn't fill the bucket very full, I could manage. I had the first window finished in seconds, it was easy work. I apparently got as far as the side of the conservatory. I say apparently because I don't remember how I got there. I also don't remember how I got to being on the floor, looking into Diane's face. "You've had a fall," she said, "the Ambulance is on its way."

"Why does my head hurt?" I asked

"You've had a fall" she explained "and hit your head on the wall. Don't you remember, I've told you several times already." She hadn't, I would have remembered that.

"Let's get you a bit more comfortable, Do you think we could get you onto the bench?"

"No problem I replied, just lift me on. Why does my head hurt?"

I'm not sure how but Diane managed to heave me onto the bench, and we sat together.

"I think that's the ambulance now," she said

"Why does my head hurt?" I asked

She sounded a little exasperated. "Don't you remember you've had a fall. I've told you several times already." Of course, she hadn't mentioned that before, but why does she keep asking me if I remember. Perhaps I should ask the paramedics to take a look at her, she was clearly having some sort of psychotic memory failure.

The two paramedics opened the back gate and came down the path each carrying a bag. They introduced themselves, but I don't remember their names. The truth is that I don't know which memories about the day are mine and which I have reclaimed from what I have been told. I don't even remember whether they were male or female, perhaps there was one of each.

The first paramedic asked what I had been up to. I wasn't sure, but it seemed like a good time to ask why my head was hurting.

The second proposed that I had had a fall. At last, I thought, why didn't anyone tell me before.

"Did you go unconscious?" the first paramedic asked while the second was busy attaching a machine to my arm.

"I think I might..." I started, but Diane interjected to say that I definitely had.

"Why does my head hurt?" I asked as a blood pressure cuff tightened around my arm.

The paramedic turned to Diane "Is he confused, or is he always like this?" She responded to the effect that the elevator doesn't always go quite as far as the top floor, but I was more confused than usual. "He keeps asking the same question, again and again," she added.

This seemed an unnecessary libel. My questions had been precise, pertinent and clear. At that moment, one just popped into my head.

"Why does my head hurt?" I asked.

The first paramedic patiently explained that I had had a fall. You see, that's all I needed to know.

He asked me to squeeze his fingers. Diane explained about my muscle wasting and that I didn't have a firm grip at the best of times. The other said she would go and get my wheelchair to wheel me round to the Ambulance because I needed to be checked out at the hospital.

Diane and the man were in conversation, presumably collecting critical medical details. Diane laughed "He is friends with one of Dan's teacher's". I still don't know how on earth Diane found out in a couple of minutes of conversation, she would make an excellent private investigator.

Diane said "Emily heard you fall and saw you on the ground. She's been great and I think she's OK. Mom and Dad are coming over to look after her."

I transferred to the chair and was pushed round to the front of the house. Two men that I had never seen before were standing in the doorway, Diane thanked them and handed them money. I was too busy to do anything about it, but I made a note to take this up with Diane later. She had just been scammed, she had given money to two strangers just because they said that they had laid a carpet and asked if there was anything they could do to help.

As one paramedic pushed me into the Ambulance, my in-laws arrived and jumped out of the car.

"Do you recognise these people?" he asked. The opportunity to claim that I had never seen them before appealed, but I replied "It's my in-laws... Hi Gill. What are you doing here? Why does my head hurt?"

"He recognises his Mother-in-law" he replied chuckling.

Soon Diane and I were riding down the street towards the hospital. At A & E, we were taken into a cubicle, and we waited to be seen. After a short time, a nurse came and asked me some questions. I asked her why I had a bad head, and she gave me some paracetamol.

A young doctor followed and sent me for a CT scan. I was wheeled off on the bed to the scanner and put through the doughnut-shaped machine, before returning to the cubicle. Diane pointed out that I was getting two black eyes and found her pocket mirror to show me. I looked like a panda.

It wasn't long before the doctor returned. He explained that I had a bleed on my brain following my fall. This was the reason for my black eyes, they are a typical symptom of a blow to the back of the head. It would probably fix itself, but they needed to keep an eye on me for a time, so they would keep me in hospital. They would find me a bed on the ward.

"Why does my head hurt?" I asked. The doctor explained that it is entirely typical after head injuries to repetitively ask the same question. I pointed out to Diane how lucky she was that I didn't have this symptom, and for some reason, she seemed to bristle a little bit.

"What happened, why does my head hurt?" I asked her.

Diane read this passage, and according to her, it wasn't entirely accurate. Apparently, we spent over six hours in A&E and every minute or so I would ask why my head hurt.

Although as I have very few faults, she does have a tendency to exaggerate them. She maintains that she wasn't bristling when I asked her "At that point," she said "I would have cheerfully throttled you!"

It was a new hospital, and I had a single room, very comfortable. I was given painkillers, but I just wanted to sleep. I slept much of the next two days. After each painkiller, I would get a couple of hours of sleep until the pain increased, and I would wait for the upcoming tablet time.

I woke up to find our neighbour had entered my room. She had brought a bag of clothes after she had thoughtfully offered Diane help. I was grateful for her kindness and apologised that I wasn't looking my best. Coincidently she was visiting her uncle had fallen the same day while mowing the lawn and was on the same ward.

After a couple of days, I was able to take a shower, and I was feeling much better. After the doctor's round, I was discharged and phoned Diane to pick me up. A short while later Diane came to collect me, I was asleep in bed and wasn't ready.

"Are you sure you are ready to come out, you still look a mess," said Diane. I explained how much better I felt, so we packed things up and left.

It was nice to be home, and we had tea, and I went to bed. At about 5 in the morning, I started being sick, several times, and I felt really dreadful. Daniel found me an orange plastic bucket from the shed. It had recently been used for moving some muddy soil so wasn't the cleanest bucket. Diane immediately phoned the ward and asked what she should do. She arranged for the neighbours to keep an eye on Emily and set off with Daniel and me back to the hospital.

In the car park, Daniel strongly suggested that I should leave the muddy bucket and ask for a sick bowl. I felt terrible, but a little comfort from keeping my head buried in the bucket, so there was no way that I was letting go of it.

We were shown to a cubicle, and we waited. Daniel found me a sick bowl, and with evident discomfort, Diane and Daniel returned the mucky bucket through the waiting rooms and put it in the car. When they returned, I had dropped off with the sick bowl resting on my head like a hat. Apparently, Dan's embarrassed discomfort grew, and he tried to remove the cardboard dish, but Diane said that it was better to leave me to sleep.

After a short time, the cubicle was visited by a nurse, she asked a few questions, and now half-awake, I gave quick, terse responses. She was kind with the confidence that comes from years of experience and efficiently ascertained what she needed to know. She found me some tablets to relieve nausea, asked if I would like some pain relief and gave me an injection.

Moments later, I started to feel some relief and become more aware of my surroundings. Soon I was wide awake and feeling better. No, not just better, I was feeling fantastic. I felt so alive and alert. Everything was so much brighter than I could remember, a world of colours, including some that were unknown to me. Throughout my life, their existence had previously gone unnoticed.

"Wow," I said "that feels great, what is that, you can give me some of that anytime. You are always welcome at my house if you bring some of that with you." I could see Daniel squirm, he gets very uncomfortable when I am at risk of embarrassing him. I ignored him as nothing was farther from my mind.

The nurse explained that it was just intravenous paracetamol, but as it goes straight into a vein, the effects are immediate.

"You are an angel" I pointed out honestly. I considered that her miraculous abilities were worthy of further compliments "A wonderful, wingless angel. Your uniform is so beautiful, it really suits you." By this time Daniel is really cringing uncomfortably. Diane was giggling, and the nurse left the cubicle, smiling to get some fresh dressings.

"Dad stop it, " Daniel rebuked as soon as the curtains closed behind her, "it's like your flirting and its really embarrassing." Diane was still giggling as the nurse returned. "It's just the drugs," she told Dan. Colours were already fading, and I started to feel tired again, but for the moment, the headache had gone. I was taken to the big doughnut machine for another CT scan. I slept through much of this time, occasionally waking, each time my bed would be in a different place. The last time I awoke to find I was in a ward of six people with Diane and Daniel sitting next to my bed.

"You are here for a while," said Diane.

My routine for the next few days was to take painkillers, sleep, wake up with a headache, and for the next few hours my sole thoughts were counting down until I could have the next dose of painkillers. My five other roommates chatted and laughed with each other. I ignored them and was happy that they ignored me. Their families would visit and joyfully exchange greetings and experiences. Diane would arrive at each visiting time, I would greet her, and she would sit tolerantly while I slept or ignored her in my self-absorbed world.

After four days, I sat up in bed, my roommates noticed a change in my demeanour and immediately included me in their conversations. After taking painkillers, I still had a headache, but life was more reasonable for an hour or two. The other occupants had all been in the ward a few more days than me. They hadn't been excluding me from their conversations, they had all experienced brain trauma and understood my need to sleep and withdraw into my own world for a while. It was release day for one of them, moving into some form of social care, so I didn't get to know him before he was on his way out of the door. Within an hour, the bed was filled with another sleeping body. I realised that he wouldn't be up to banter or light conversation for a few days, so let him sleep.

Opposite me was George. He was a kind and humorous man in his seventies and had led a fit and active life. While out for a bike ride and had fallen off when a car cut in too close. George's family explained that he hadn't been wearing a helmet and had been severely injured, so it had taken him some time to get this far.

"Be careful Matron's coming, she's very scary," George said in a cheeky stage whisper from his bed, well within matron's hearing.

A commanding voice rose from the doorway "Is everyone wearing their socks?" She looked around the room for affirmation "George knows what the punishment is for anyone who isn't, there will be trouble." said Matron, playing along with a smile.

She carried on down the corridor to berate the next ward. I looked around and noticed that those who had their feet on top of their sheets were wearing surgical stockings. No one had mentioned wearing stockings to me, so I happily assumed that Matron's stern words didn't apply to me, but now I started to wonder. Soon afterwards, a young nurse came round to check my blood pressure, so I asked about the socks. He discreetly went and found me a pair and levered them onto my big feet.

George had a mischievous streak and would recount amusing gossip about everyone on the ward. One nurse had inherited a circus, although it was past its former glory days and they recently had to retire the arthritic acrobats and geriatric clowns. The cleaner's hobby was grooming her alpacas and apparently she sheared their fur like poodles. When I asked the male nurse why he had quit his job as a long-distance lorry driver, I came to wonder about the sources and accuracy of George's inside info.

Each visiting time Georges family would kindly ask us all if George had been causing any trouble, disregarding his protests of innocence. Invariably Matron would pay a visit to rebuke George and join in the laughing at his latest escapades.

Next to George was Bob. He was recovering from a brain tumour operation. A railway signalman who had worked on railways since leaving school. He worked in a signal box that I regularly passed when I used to travel to London by train. Bob had given his working life to being a signalman and knew his job, as well as any virtuoso knows theirs. I had never given much thought to how trains operate, so I was fascinated by Bob's explanation of the intricacies of keeping railway engines and the passengers safely on different tracks. I was pleased that on rail journeys my life had been in the hands of people like Bob. I hoped that they had great replacements for operating the signals and points in Bob's absence. Bob had been in hospital for a few weeks and was visited each day by his obviously devoted and proud wife.

The day after I was discharged from the hospital, my GP gave me a call. He had received the paperwork from the hospital and wanted to know if I needed any pain relief. In a hurry to discharge me, the hospital had neglected to give me a prescription for the medication to stop queasiness. He arranged for the chemist to dispense some for me and so I was delighted he called. He also told me that he would put me on a short rehabilitation programme and soon I was being visited each midday during the week by a care worker. This reassured Diane that someone would check that I was OK while she was at work. I was told that they would make me a hot drink, talk to me and watch me make a sandwich. They emphasised that they needed to see me making the sandwich before they could go. After a few days I was well enough to make packed lunches for Diane, Dan and Emily before they left in the morning, but I had to wait for the arrival of the care worker before I could make mine. They were kind but busy people and often didn't arrive until mid-afternoon. By noon I had already felt hungry and made myself a sandwich, so when they came, I created and consumed my second lunch.

Diane and I decided that we needed to invest in a telecare system. She would have the reassurance that I would be able to get help if I fell when she was out. In the early 1970s, Wilhelm Hormann had a brilliant idea. He developed a pendant was worn around the neck that, when pressed, sent a signal to a machine that was attached to a rotary phone. The phone would send a pre-programmed message to a predetermined number. The principle hasn't changed although the technology is sleeker. Within days a system was installed, and when they reviewed the rehabilitation programme after a couple of weeks, I felt that they had served their purpose and asked them to end the visits.

As time progressed the pain in my head was easing so that there would be more extended periods before I would withdraw waiting for the next relief from pain.

As things slowly returned to normal, we thought about what could have happened, and so Diane and I discussed what could be done to help prevent another head injury. I was banned from walking around the side of the house until we had the gravel removed and pavers laid so that I could go in my wheelchair. We found a new window cleaner who would also clean our conservatory. I also looked for a hat that would protect my head. All I could find were hats for epilepsy that had been solely designed for function so looked very medical.

After some searching, I discovered that various products have been developed that work in addition to helmets and are designed to protect the skulls of baseball and American football players.

The one I liked was made out of a jelly-like sheets. The sales video was brilliant. A shouty man, like some down market second-hand car dealer advert, described the benefits while covering his hand with a sheet and bashing it with a heavy metal bar. He got more shouty as the video went on and bashed his hand harder and harder without any apparent damage or pain. Of course, I had to send for one. I was delighted when it arrived and went off in search of a hammer. Re-enacting the video. I tentatively hit my hand and it felt fine, so I gave it a harder hit. I was pleased that I didn't rush in full power because it hurt. It hurt quite a lot. Perhaps that was why the man was so shouty. Never the less I hadn't damaged my hand, and it was clear that it did give a lot of protection. The cap was very close-fitting, so I intended to wear it under another hat. I have a ridiculously large head, I have always assumed it is proportional to brainpower, but then I have no evidence of this. With my new cap, it was a size bigger. It seems that British shops don't cater to people with big heads and so I had to buy a hat from an American online shop. It's right, things are bigger in America. It was ideal, perhaps looking a little odd, but so far it has worked.

CHAPTER 16

MY BLACK SAUSAGE DOG

Sir John Eric Erichsen, was apparently an excellent looking surgeon who was well regarded internationally and Queen Victoria's surgeon-extraordinary. An unusual job title and I have no idea what was so surprising about him compared to her other surgeons. It seems that the Queen liked him and made him a Baronet in 1895.

Sir John studied the symptoms people experienced following concussion and head trauma. He found that many people experienced depression and suggested this was due to "molecular disarrangement" to the spine. Depression had been noted in injured railroad workers and was initially called "railroad spine". Others suggested that the symptoms were hysteria or just feigned and labelled the persisting symptoms "compensation neurosis" brought about by the railroad's custom of compensating workers who had been injured.

It wasn't until World War I that there was a greater understanding that concussion and trauma lead to a range of puzzling psychological symptoms.

When I was younger mental illness wasn't talked about. People who had suffered nervous breakdowns disappeared for a long time. A man down out street had one, but I never understood what it was. I assumed that he was found rampaging naked through the streets with a bucket on his head shouting "Muffins", or he had buried his wife up to her neck in the rose bed, dressed in a bikini while singing the national anthem. No one would talk about it or what it was. It seems these days people are too depressed to have nervous breakdowns. There wasn't much about mental illness on the television other than jokes and mockery. I can only think of one positive, or at least not wholly negative, depiction, Howling Mad Murdock in the A-Team, although perhaps he slightly oversold the benefits.

I don't think that my mood changed throughout the process of realising something was wrong with my body to being diagnosed. I knew from the beginning that the likely options were not good news, so when I was diagnosed, I felt that it was relatively easy to accept, actually it was a relief. Things could have been much worse.

Just knowing the name of the condition meant that I could research it on the internet and even make connections with others with the same situation. I actually found it fascinating to learn about the biological processes involved, the ideas that had been proposed for treatments and those that had failed in medical trials. It also connected me with random people around the world. I discovered that IBM is so cool that it has its own country song "I Won't Stand for That" sung by Mike Shirk who lived with IBM and wrote a blog about his experiences until the end.

Being a little nosy, I equally enjoyed exploring parts of hospitals that I would have no cause to see otherwise, and the equipment was brilliant, each piece invented by some genius. Some ultra high tech and others mystical contraptions held together with gaffer tape. There were losses and things that I could no longer do, but there was still so much that I could do. My mindset changed, no point in having ambitions for things I couldn't achieve. I had time to consider what I wanted to do. The future would look after itself, I didn't have to spend time worrying about it.

Not being able to do anything in the hospital gave me a lot of time to think. I set myself a task of making lists in my head of good things that life had given, and despite the pain, I felt positive.

I made mental lists of the dates that Diane and I had been on, I made a long list the things she had done or said that made me laugh, the friends I knew and loved at different times in my life. I listed the pets that I had owned, the cars I owned, the restaurants we had been to, young women that I had dated and kissed when I was a young man (and before I met Diane), the places in the UK and overseas that we had been to on holiday.

I tried to recall as many of the lovely people I had worked with and the countries and amazing places that work had taken me to. There are some periods, perhaps an hour, a day or a week, that I could recall with total clarity and other periods, maybe years, that seem to have drifted out of recollection.

I was amazed by how much information I was able to retrieve, information that has lost its relevance years ago is tucked away in my skull. Almost all of it is hopeless garbage, but bedded in them are memories that made me smile. For all practical purposes, this information is practically pointless. Why does my brain think that it is vital to immediately remember the colour of some fence posts I once passed on a lazy Sunday walk thirty years ago when it can't bring to mind anything remotely important such as people's names, at the right time? The information is in my head just buried so deeply, tucked underneath piles of neurones and behind oodles of random recollections. I could be speaking with someone I know quite well, and it won't be until a day later in the middle of something completely unrelated that my mind exclaims "That was Gordon." I worry if I get dementia, how will anyone tell?

Physically I was fine, but something strange was happening in my head. I still had those happy lists in my head, but real life is messy, and sometimes tragic and sad things happen alongside some of the happy times. Suddenly memories of a period of my life when I was aged 21, started to replay in my mind until they became overwhelming.

I remembered my 21st birthday party, a happy gathering of friends and family. The party was missing one friend, Angus.

A group of us had been friends since childhood and together, we had discovered the forbidden pleasures of adulthood, including drinking, smoking and girls. Angus was a really terrible driver, and I vowed never to be his passenger. We all told him that unless he slowed down, he would kill himself, but to be fair, none of us were very good at accepting advice at that age. Angus didn't slow down and inevitably was killed crashing into a tree.

I already had some experience of car crashes, I had been almost killed when I was thrown out of the back window of a car as it crashed into a hedge and was thrown onto its roof. The vehicle had been driven too fast by a friend when we were late getting to a golf tournament. We never got there, but we were all alive, if bruised and cut. I had a trip home in an ambulance. On another occasion, Dad was driving us back one dark night from a day trip to Bakewell when we were flagged down. The man had somehow managed to escape unhurt from a car that had destroyed a telegraph pole. The Mini Estate was crushed into about half its volume, but inside someone was alive and shouting. In the dark, Dad, a doctor, tried to assess how to give first aid but realised that the limb he was holding didn't belong to the shouting man, but to the dead driver. We tried to move contorted metal panels to make some space so that Dad could help the trapped survivor, but all our efforts were reasonably ineffectual. Being a remote country field, it took some time before the welcome arrival of Fire, Police and Ambulances who were quickly able to extricate the unfortunate passenger minus his legs.

Not long after my 21st birthday, my wonderful and lovable Granny died. Within the year, on my way home, I arrived at Crewe station and was met by my sister and the local vicar with news of Dad's death. He collapsed a few hours previously clearing leaves in the garden. Shortly afterwards, I was cut from my short career as a Royal Navy pilot when they cottoned on that their aircraft and by extension, the safety of the country, were not safe in my hands. When I left the Navy, it naturally had an impact on my confidence, Dad would have known what to say, and I missed not being able to talk with him.

Surprisingly this was also a year when I had beautiful memories, and I clearly remember the friendships. It was the year a group of us, four friends from university, invented mud skiing, much like water skiing, but on estuary mud, being towed behind a small boat tender with a tiny outboard. It was the year we also discovered that estuary mud is almost impossible to wash off. I had learned to dive while I was at University and relearned to do things the Navy way, which I loved. My uncle was a judge, and when I left the Navy, he invited me to do a few weeks work as a judges marshal. These days if judges have marshals they are usually trainee barristers, as it offers the opportunity to view the justice system operating from the inside, and to watch advocates practising their profession from the vantage point of the judge's bench. It is just a ceremonial post, and in addition to excellent board and lodging, I was paid £2.10 a day. It wasn't until I started in the role that I learned that the marshal's prime purpose was to go into the court in front of the judge in case there was an attempt on his life.

At the time, I was young and resilient, with the philosophy to get on with life for good and bad. Now though, all the beautiful things were the faded memories from over half a lifetime ago, while every painful memory seemed clearly etched in my mind, as clearly and in as much detail as if it had just happened.

My mind replayed events constantly as if they happened yesterday. It wasn't just significant traumatic events that I remembered. I also remembered times I had inadvertently caused offence, or my stupidity had put someone out. Really ridiculous things, I remembered telling a joke that was met with a bewildered and uncomfortable silence. Not an offensive joke, just not funny. I don't know why this would stick in my mind. At home, it is a daily occurrence that my jokes are met with a jaded silence. I am happy chuckling to myself. I also remembered a middle-aged lady who called me a rude man after I didn't hold open a door which swung in her face. I don't think that I had seen her, but I probably should have taken more care. I know rationally that it was really trivial, it was hardly Crimewatch material, and no one else, not even the unknown lady, would remember the incident. I had never thought about it until for some reason, it violently erupted to the surface from somewhere deep in my mind. I suddenly felt a level of extreme self-consciousness that I was unaware of at the time. I didn't know why this and other trivial incidents gained so much importance in my mind.

The subjects of my remorse had all happened over 30 years ago, and if they had caused offence would have been long forgotten and easily forgiven. My rational mind also knew that I will have done things that were far more hurtful at other times, perhaps unintentionally or out of stupidity, that has been long resolved or forgotten. My mind has filed these memories under lessons learned and forgotten.

The memories constantly came, like having a switch that wouldn't turn off in my head. The same events would run over and over in my head, like a crazy tape on constant loop. I could reason about each incident but it didn't stop the repetitious movie playing between my ears. From morning to night, whatever I was doing, eating, talking, cooking, watching TV the tape would be playing. The only relief was being asleep, but if I woke to go to the toilet, the tape started instantly and ran and ran until eventually, I would fall back to sleep again. On the positive side, whenever I was awake, it would give Diane some respite from my snoring.

I'm not good at multitasking. If I am focused on something, it is difficult to get my attention. It doesn't have to be something significant that I find so distracting. Diane knows about this phenomenon with much frustration. She once asked me to pick up some dry cleaning, I set off with my daughter, and we decided as we were doing such an excellent job we would stop at the sweet shop for a treat. When we returned home, we had considerately bought a tasty treat for Diane, but forgotten the dry cleaning.

It was next to impossible to concentrate on anything with the incessant noise of my thoughts. Everything seemed more difficult, so I did less, got more grumpy than usual and generally lost interest. I realised that this wasn't good and decided that I needed to get my act together. I had no idea how, so it eventually came to me that I could ask my GP if there were any local counselling services. Fortunately, I already had an appointment booked for another reason, so I decided to ask the question at that visit. I hadn't spoken to Diane because I didn't know how to explain my feelings, and it seemed unnecessary to add an additional burden.

My visit was with an unfortunate locum GP. She dealt with the purported purpose of the visit kindly and professionally. I started to put my coat on and casually asked if there were counselling services that I could contact or be referred to. She said, "Why do you ask that question?"

Oh my god! For some reason, I hadn't thought she would ask me that, I felt that I would be given a number to call or a place to go. I started to explain my intrusive thoughts, but like a bursting, a dam a tidal wave of emotion overwhelmed me, and amongst my tears, I could only burble a few incomprehensible sentences.

"Oh Jon," the locum said with evident sincerity "you are depressed. I need a little time to help, make an appointment at reception to see me tomorrow."

Until this point, I hadn't considered that I was depressed. I thought that I was going a little bonkers, but depression simply hadn't occurred to me. I thought that being depressed means feeling low or sad. There have been times in my life when I have felt sad, achingly sad. It is a painful part of life that at times we lose people and pets we love. We were desperately sad when we lost Toby, our lovely family cat. It was a sadness that we all shared. We could console each other sharing memories of him stretching his paw through the bannisters to ambush you as you walked down the hall, playfully chasing light reflections until he would collapse exhausted or watching snooker on the television.

For me, there were significant distinctions between sadness and depression. The times when I was sad, I understood why I was miserable. The pain was acute but could be shared with others. Kind words offer some analgesic relief, and amongst the pain, happy memories and warm recollections still give pleasure. Gradually the pain of the sadness eases, and you are left with happy memories.

Depression crept up gradually, and I didn't consciously recognise that I was depressed or why I was feeling miserable. It wasn't that the pain of depression was acute, although as I discovered at the doctors, whenever I tried to verbalise my feelings, I would be overwhelmed by a tidal wave of emotion.

The sheer quantity of detail going round my head was a surprise. I could clearly recall locations, colours, sounds, and even smells. Unfortunately, it was all totally pointless information, not a fact that might just come in useful in a pub quiz, not even something that might form a conversation, just mental rubbish. If I had used this storage space in my brain to store useful facts, I could have earned numerous doctorates and professorships. Unfortunately, it was just crap. Each intrusive memory was linked with feelings at least as intense as if it had just happened.

I was lucky. I was given medication that helped and went for weekly counselling sessions. For ten weeks, the counsellor got me to watch her finger move backwards and forwards using a treatment called Eye Movement Desensitization and Reprocessing. I was told that usually during sleep, your brain processes your experiences. It gradually peels away the emotions and files away the information as just another memory. Apparently, my problem was that these thoughts were stuck in the most primitive parts of the brain. The moving finger supposedly replicates what your eyes do during sleep, helping your mind to do it's sorting. Naturally, I was cynical not least because I wasn't sure that my brain had anything other than primitive parts, but by the end of my treatment, the intrusiveness of the thoughts and intensity of feelings had subsided.

Churchill supposedly characterised his depression as "my black dog, a faithful companion, sometimes out of sight, but always returning." Perhaps it was a Bulldog, but considering the weight of worries on his shoulders, I imagine he envisioned something bigger like a Mastiff. My depression was mild, I always felt that I still had some control over life, I knew that I had the love and support of Diane and the family, and I never thought of ending things. I thought of my depression as an annoying miniature black sausage dog.

Perhaps it would have helped to know that depression is prevalent after brain injury. Since Sir John's first observations, there have been lots of studies, and it seems that about half of people recovering from brain injuries experience depression and loss of motivation during the first year. As a consequence, many find that they are increasingly isolated and have relationship difficulties. Unfortunately for many their black dogs are too big and too fierce, and they find even asking for help and participating in their rehabilitation too tricky. I'm pleased my faithful companion was a sausage dog.

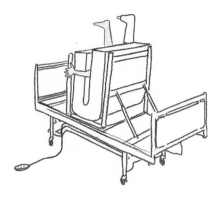

CHAPTER 17

BACK UP THE CREEK

The residents of Salford Towers would recognise Chris Saggers. As their window cleaner, he would regularly wash their windows before slowly and deliberately moving on down to the next flat. One day though residents would have seen Mr Saggers face for just a fraction of a second as he passed by their windows much, much faster than usual. He had been working on scaffolding cleaning the windows on the 22nd floor, had lost his footing and started his rapid deadly drop towards the ground. Residents rushed to look out with the expectation of witnessing the gory remains of poor Mr Saggers splattered across their car park. Instead, he was already standing and dusting himself off calling up, "I'm fine." One of the residents will have noticed a big dent in the roof of their car. Mr Saggers was lucky the resident parked in such a fortuitous place. The car's owner may have had other views but was perhaps consoled that they had saved Mr Saggers from certain death and there was no need to find a new window cleaner.

Mr Saggers walked away from a fall of 22 storeys, but this was a mere tumble compared to the story of Nicholas Alkemade. He was cheerfully flying over Germany when his day was about to take a turn for the worse. Some German fighter pilots took exception to Nicholas, probably because he was flying a Lancaster bomber plane and had sprinkled its deadly exploding cargo over the Fatherland. The Germans decided to perforate his plane with lead while shouting "Achtung Got in Himmel". I know this fact because in the comic books I read as a child, German pilots always shouted "Achtung Got in Himmel" on encountering the enemy. If that wasn't bad enough for Nicholas, one bullet hit his fuel tank and turned his bomber into a flaming inferno. He was now being cremated inside a flying metal coffin and heading rapidly towards self burial in the earth below. Nicholas had the presence of mind to open the emergency hatch and jump into the black void, but if he thought that was in any way an improvement to his situation, he was mistaken. He immediately passed out due to the lack of oxygen and plummeted like one of his bombs towards the earth 18,000 feet below. He never got the chance to pull his ripcord, but if he had, it wouldn't have made a difference as the inferno had incinerated his parachute. At this point, his odds of survival looked worse than a bet on Muffin the Mule winning the Grand National.

Quickly Nicolas would have reached his terminal velocity of perhaps 200 miles an hour and was heading rapidly towards a dense forest and certain impalement on a pine tree. This is where his luck improved, being unconscious his muscles were relaxed, and he had the remarkable fortune of passing between the trees and being slowed down by the layers of pine branches before finally landing in a vast snowdrift cushioning his fall further.

He was quickly captured and interviewed by the Gestapo, who were by nature a sceptical lot. When his plane was discovered it confirmed his story and his captors, so impressed he had jumped without his parachute, gave him a certificate, and he became something of a celebrity while living out the war in a POW camp.

Chris Saggers and Nicholas Alkemade fell a cumulative total of over 18,120 feet and between them sustained no more injuries than a small cut, a hairline elbow fracture and a sprained ankle.

On the other hand, I fell from the dizzy height of 17 garden peas and broke both the tibia and fibula bones in my ankle. My knee gave way as I was stepping off the 3-inch step next to our front door. This isn't the only time I have injured myself and sustained broken bones and cuts that needed stitching, but most of the others were from ground level.

Diane was home and rushed to me. After finding that I wasn't too severely hurt, she brought the Camel out. I lay on it, and she inflated it so that I gently rose to a sitting position. I tried to get up, but my ankle was too painful, so I transferred to my manual wheelchair and Diane heaved me up the doorstep and into the house. At this point, it wasn't much different from many other falls. I often sprain my ankles when I fall, and I think it is partly due to my splints. I was fine and felt no different from previous occasions.

Diane had a crucial meeting in the afternoon, which she wanted to cancel and take me to Accident and Emergency. I insisted that I was fine so reluctantly she left me confined to my chair, with painkillers, a drink (and a urine bottle), phones, personal alarms and something mindless on the television. She kissed me and said she would be back as soon as she could. I watched telly and snoozed. When I woke up, the programme had changed, and a shouty man called Jeremy Kyle was on. It was quickly apparent that it was his show. He mentioned it quite a few times, and there was a large Jeremy Kyle Show sign behind him. It wasn't really my sort of thing, so I looked for the control to find a documentary. Where was the remote? I tried feeling around the seat behind me. Bother, not there. I then noticed it on the television stand. I had no chance of reaching it, so I sat back and watched some more of Mr Kyle's show. There had been an advert break, and the show restarted with the by-line "Bringing People Together". Unfortunately, the people he brought together obvious hated each other's guts and would have been quite happy to fight out their differences.

An enormous mound of muscle called Steve had the job of standing between them, and the two parties seemed quite content to hurl insults at each other from opposite sides of Steve. It became difficult to understand what was going on because there was an awful lot of bleeping. This show must be the dream job and career pinnacle for bleep button operators. The audience had scented blood and were braying and whooping like over-excited hyenas. It transpired that the guest's boyfriend was a serial BLEEPer and had BLEEPed with other former best friends. As he had already admitted several previous occasions, it seemed to be more an argument about the maths than rights and wrongs. Besides, it transpired that the guest wasn't entirely innocent and had BLEEPS of her own. The upshot was that all the parties agreed to never see each other again and the show drew to its conclusion replaying the joyful jingle "Bringing People Together".

I slept in my chair downstairs that night as my ankle was painful and I couldn't get onto the stairlift. It was only in the morning that it was clear that things were not right. I still couldn't put any weight on my foot, and horrible blisters had grown on my ankle. Diane insisted on taking me to Accident and Emergency, and I agreed.

When we arrived at the Accident and Emergency Unit, I wasn't the only injured person waiting. Every day in the UK about 1,000 people fall and are admitted to Accident and Emergency Units. Falls are the most significant cause of emergency hospital admissions for older people. This costs a lot of money which could be used to strategically place 17 million mattresses placed to prevent injury from falling. I should be a politician, but like any idea by Chris Grayling, Transport Minister, perhaps I haven't thought it through thoroughly.

After a brief consultation, I was sent for some X rays. The radiologist asked me to transfer onto the table from my wheelchair. I have not yet visited an X-ray department with a transfer board, so moving onto the X-ray table means parking the chair as near as possible and heaving my bum over the gap. Without the use of one ankle, this is even more difficult. The radiologist was a no-fuss type and painfully placed my leg into different positions for each picture. She took a lot of images, and I was a little concerned about how much radiation was targeted at my crotch, although I could see the benefit for nocturnal toilet visits with of a pair of glowing testicles.

It transpired that I had broken both my Tibia and Fibula so it was unsurprising that I couldn't walk. The young doctor had recently arrived from another hospital where bone fractures are a speciality and took an interest in every detail. This was comforting for me but frustrating for the nurses whose practice was scrutinised at every stage.

They gave me some drugs, I don't know what drugs they were, but they seemed to work as the doctor repositioned the bones and my leg was put into a temporary plaster.

The fracture was not weight-bearing, so it was clear that I wouldn't be out and about for some time. This raised a few practical problems, and the doctor explained that I would need a care package. Diane and I were taken to an office where a helpful physiotherapist and occupational therapist discussed the options with us. One option would be to remain in hospital, but hospitals are not the best places to be as they are full of bugs, besides I would be taking up valuable bed space. The main difficulty about going home was that I wouldn't be able to transfer onto the stairlift and so I couldn't go upstairs. This meant that I would need a bed downstairs. I wouldn't be able to get to the toilet, so I would need a commode and I would need a transfer board to get on and off it. They had to do a bit of wrangling to get a bed, but very soon they had arranged for all this to be delivered and set up later that day. A hospital social worker was meant to be at the meeting, they had paged him several times without response. Eventually, he arrived and stood in the doorway behind me.

"He will need a care package morning, lunchtime and night," he said to Diane. I couldn't see him, and I had hoped he would have introduced himself, but at least he sounded helpful. "What is your key-safe number?"

Diane replied, "We don't know, we will tell you later." Diane knew it of course but wasn't going to tell someone she had met for less than a minute. He might as well ask for her pin number.

"Well, how do you get in then!" He sounded a bit pleased with his response. The physiotherapist responded incredulously "I expect she has a key of her own, this lady is Mr McVey's wife."

The put down didn't seem to register with the social worker. "I suppose we can deal with that later," he responded. He went on to outline what the carers would be doing at each visit. Diane asked if we needed so much care in the morning and evening as she was happy to provide the care he had outlined at those times. As she would be at work, we would need a carer to come in at lunchtimes.

Ignoring her, he said "let's start with the full package and see how we go. It will cost about £500 a week."

I still hadn't seen the social worker's face, apart for a partial reflection in the window, but I had come to the conclusion that I didn't like him. I thought I would disillusion him of the impression he seemed to have that I was unable to speak, and so I asked him if the care was free.

"Oh no," he said "you wouldn't qualify for any funding. If you were able to weight bear, you would be eligible for a rehabilitation fund, but as you can't, there is nothing" The logic of this statement totally escaped me, so I sought clarification.

"You mean that I would be eligible for free care if I could walk, but as my needs are greater, it isn't free," he confirmed this was the case. "And you want to spend our money on a full care package, costing a small fortune instead of just the lunchtimes we need." I decided that even though I had only met him a few minutes, still hadn't seen his face or knew his name, I really didn't like this man.

At this point, his training kicked in, and he realised that the situation was turning hostile and so we agreed that we would arrange my care with the care agencies directly.

Shortly after arriving home, the bed and other items came and were set up in our dining room. I had a control enabling me to raise my head, my legs, or tilt the bed. It is possibly a man thing, but I could get hours of enjoyment, seeing how high my legs would go, how far I could lower my head and if I pressed both buttons together I could squash myself up like a sandwich filling. My ankle was very swollen, so there was a need to keep it raised. I have to thank Dr William D. Gatch for my fun and for making my ankle more comfortable. People died in Victorian times from flatbeds. In 1909 Dr Gatch invented the adjustable bed that enabled patients to sit up or raise their feet so that swelling and wounds would drain correctly.

Over the following weeks, we arranged for carer workers to come in each day when Diane was at work. Over the weeks there were many different carers, many came several times and a few only once. Without exception, they were kind, friendly and professional. Each day they would walk through the door and literally not seeing my best side, would carry out tasks of personal nature while making conversation.

One day the care worker was unable to open the door with our key. I could talk with her through the window, but none of my suggestions worked. My walking stick was next to the bed, and I managed to hook the empty commode and drag it next to me. There I had to lock the wheels so that I could transfer across and then unlock them, again using the handle of my walking stick as a lever. Now I could wheel my way out of the dining room down the hall. It was the first time she had been greeted at the front door by someone seated on a toilet, but care workers are made of strong stuff, and she didn't flinch.

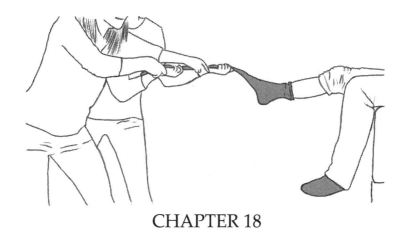

CHAPTER 18

COMPRESSION SOCKS

I fell on a night time trip to the toilet and ended up sitting on my calf. My leg was bent at the knee, not in at an odd angle, but I was sitting on it, and it was agonising. I had woken Diane up from deep sleep, and after momentary bewilderment, she got out of bed to help me. I wasn't very coherent, but I had made it clear enough that I needed my leg to be moved from under me. Diane managed to heave it out. My ankle hurt, but my knee was agony. I had done something similar before and so knew that I had a hyperflexion injury, where the knee joint is forced to extend beyond its normal range painfully damaging the ligaments: In my experience, this is my least favourite injury because the pain is constant. Broken ribs are similarly uncomfortable. Broken bones are just as painful but once set you can find comfort for some time. Not that I have a preferred injury, although I had a small fracture in my big toe, which caused no pain at all.

Quickly my knee started to swell, followed by my calf, ankle and foot. This swelling is a frequent and uncomfortable consequence of falling. Raising my foot always helps, but even after I can no longer feel the injury, the swelling remains. When at some point I put my shoes on, they no longer fit, if I can get them on at all. My leg is wedged into ankle splints with flesh swelling over the edges.

The solution is compression stockings. Hippocrates described how to treat patients with leg ulcers with tight bandages, but this was old news even then. Cave drawings in the Sahara show soldiers bandaging their lower legs at least two thousand years before.

A little more recently in the 16th century, Ambrose Paré did his bit. He was a barber-surgeon to French kings and perhaps better known for conducting an experiment to test the belief that bezoar stones were an antidote to any poison. Bezoar stones are disagreeable polished masses formed in the gut from partly digested food and hair. I cannot imagine how anyone first thought that these might help counteract a glass of hemlock. A cook had been sentenced to hang for stealing cutlery. Ambrose instead arranged for her to take poison and the cook agreed, with the hope that Ambrose was wrong and swallowing a bezoar stone would save her. Unfortunately for the cook, Ambrose was proved right, and she died.

Ambrose also wrote about an Italian woman, Dorothea, who allegedly gave birth to undecaplets (apparently the word for a multiple birth of 11 babies and not a word that you will need to use very often.) This must have been quite a shock, especially as she had previously had a multiple birth of nine babies. I imagine that the poor lady needed compression socks. Ambrose was on the case and realised that external compression helped treat slow blood flow in the lower legs.

I have several sets of compression socks that were measured to fit. They are made from industrial-grade stretchy stuff. Before they have been washed, it is a bit like trying to stretch a car tyre. With little grip in my hands, putting them on is a challenge, especially until they have been washed a few times. Fortunately, there is a gadget that helps with this, but it takes me time. The device is meant to help to take the sock off, but I have never managed to get it to work. I have found a way, gripping the toe between my walking stick and the floor, to pull them off. Sometimes it works, but the socks have the property of a Chinese Finger Lock puzzle. The harder you pull, the tighter it grips, so often I need to resort to asking Diane, Daniel and Emily to yank the sock off my foot. It's not a job they like doing, the elastic means that they tug away until the elasticated stocking catapults off in a cloud of dried skin.

Alongside compression, Manual Lymphatic Drainage is a type of massage that really helps with swollen feet. It starts at your head, which is a bit weird. It was developed by two Danes in the 1930s by Dr Emil Vodder and his wife, Dr Estrid Vodder. They developed careful hand movements that stretch and twist the skin to cause lymph movement. I was dubious, but its effects in reducing the swelling are immediate and significant.

My therapist also used a machine which uses electricity to produce a tingling sensation. I held a metal object connected to a wire. The therapist wore latex gloves which made a tingling sensation whenever she touched. The gloves were important. If she happened to accidentally brush up against my foot, she would receive a shock which I couldn't feel but would make her visibly flinch.

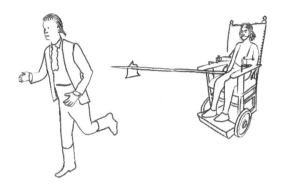

CHAPTER 19

HEADS (& WHEELCHAIRS) WILL ROLL

Sir Tomas Fairfax knew which side to butter his bread, both sides. During the English Civil War, he was Commander in Chief of the Parliamentarian Forces and noted for his for many daring military victories. We all have nicknames, Sir Thomas was called Black Tom due to his dark hair and complexion, which was much cooler than my school nickname Moose, but I won't go into the details of that.

He was a fair-minded and noble man, but his subordinate, the warty faced Oliver was a bit of a pushy git. Fairfax was content with winning the Civil War and had treated the defeated king compassionately, but Oliver was whipping up support for a show trial. The unhappy Fairfax publicly refused to take part and eventually resigned, leaving the Republic in a similar predicament to the unfortunate King Charles I, without a head. His deputy Oliver Cromwell filled the gap and was now in control.

When Cromwell died, he was briefly replaced by his incompetent son. Fairfax shrewdly realised that the tide was rapidly turning and he took an active role in the restoration of Charles II.

This was now an unhappy time for those who had been on the Parliamentarian side, especially those who had been involved in the trial and signing the death warrant of Charles's dad. Most of these found that their heads were to be fitted on spikes to decorate London Bridge. Fairfax, however, escaped these retributions and perhaps to be doubly sure that he was on the King's right side, he gave him a horse to ride to his coronation.

Sir Thomas Fairfax spent the remaining eleven years of his life quietly at his house in Yorkshire. Many biographies stop there, but his retirement years are the reason he is mentioned here. Sir John obviously lived well during these years as he developed painful and crippling gout. As a result, he acquired the latest technology for the disabled, a self-propelling wheelchair.

The chair looks like a dining chair with three large wooden wheels and a footplate. On each arm is a crank handle that rotates horizontally, one propelling the left wheel and the other the right. I'm not an engineer, but I would imagine that the gearing ratios would mean that it would take a lot of effort to move a few feet. The two cranks had the advantage that it was steerable which was useful unless Sir Thomas was weaker in one arm, in which case his final years of retirement would have been spent recounting his greatest battles while going round and round in circles.

After my first stay in hospital, we started to discuss whether I should use a wheelchair at times. If your fate is to suffer a spinal injury, then the decision is different, and the choices you have are suddenly imposed and limited. I didn't experience that trauma, I could still walk, my decline was slow, and my condition didn't change from day to day. If you had the option to walk, why would you sit in a wheelchair? Two factors affected my decision, our decision. I say our decision because using a wheelchair or not has a profound impact on the family.

There came a time when my walking was getting gradually slower and slower. Years ago, when we used to go on long walks, we would set off at what I thought was a comfortable pace. Diane used to ask me to remember that her legs were quite a lot shorter than mine, and she had to do more steps at a higher speed to cover the same distance. Now the tables were turned, I was again setting the pace but at a rate that was so slow that for Diane, it was uncomfortable and frustrating. In shops and museums, it doesn't matter that you amble from one thing to another, in most of the rest of the world it is a pain in the arse. Being in a wheelchair would mean that I could participate in family life more, not less. On the other hand, someone would need to help me with a manual wheelchair.

The next issue was safety, falling when we are out isn't much fun. After several times, people around you spend their time worrying about you. Even if nothing happened, it prevented everyone from enjoying the day. At the time we started to question whether it was worth going for a day out. It was all too clear that something had to be done and I agreed to use a wheelchair. Waiting until I couldn't walk at all would be much too late, life would have become impossible way before then.

Using a wheelchair and being able to walk, make me think of Andy, the wheelchair-using character in Little Britain who, when his carer Lou was distracted, would be out of his chair doing cartwheels and climbing ladders. In my dreams, I walk and run, climb stairs and do press-ups. When someone I know enters my dream, I remember I can't walk and dive for a wheelchair. In my nightmares, I have become Andy.

We decided to try using a wheelchair when we visited a bird sanctuary. It seemed sensible as the distances would be too far for me to walk. It was flat with good parking next to the reception and when I phoned they said that there were chairs that we could borrow. When we arrived, they had a strange collection of chairs that had been donated. Some had been adapted for people with particular needs, others needed some essential maintenance, and some were missing parts. Other carers who had arrived with infirm elderly relatives were similarly searching. The best option left appeared to be a bariatric chair, made to be extra, extra wide. I am not a lightweight, but our picnic, bags, cameras and coats fitted comfortably by my side. Diane's arms were almost at full stretch, pushing the beast of a chair. It was obviously quite a cheap chair and despite being the dimensions for a big load, the materials and build quality appeared inadequate for that purpose. It seemed to lack the necessary amount of lateral strength, so each side could move independently of the other, contorting the seat uncomfortably. The bearings had no longer had any right to hold that name. The wheels could turn, but it became clear when Diane had to push me down the long ramp out of the reception that they had long passed their ability to reduce friction. To be frank, the chair was in a worse state than I was. Its useful life was well past, and perhaps it would have been fairer for me to carry it.

Diane persevered, with occasional help from Daniel and Emily. Despite the limitations, we could see the benefits. We ate ice cream, and Diane and the children decided to hire a canoe on the lake. I obviously wasn't going and as it was a beautiful day they found me a place to sit under a tree. Perhaps I should have paid more attention to what was around me. It was beautiful and fresh under the dappled shade of the leaves, but even so, when a breeze came, it was very welcome. Well, it was very pleasant for a few moments until there was a crashing thump on my head. Seconds later, another gust was followed by a second thump. Then more and more blows. Above my head, the branch that offered the welcome shade immediately restored a natural balance of pleasure and pain by swaying in the breeze and clobbering my head. The breeze picked up, and the branch seemed able to predict wherever I moved my head. I was parked on long grass, and I didn't have the muscle power to move the chair, so I used the coats to protect my head and resigned myself to waiting for their return.

Emily hadn't enjoyed the canoe, afraid that it would capsize. For both of us, there are lessons to be learned from every experience.

By the time we visited an arboretum a few days later, we had figured out that a scooter was a better option and fortunately there was the option to borrow one. Now if you have never driven a scooter they are not challenging to drive, but I would recommend that you take instruction before you start. There are two controls that you have to take note of. The first is a dial and before you start you must decide what speed you wish to go and then turn the dial from 1 slow, to 4 very fast. Although there is a 5 on the dial, I was warned that this is only for use by Jeremy Clarkson. The second control has two leavers, one by each handle. If you pull the right-hand one, you go forward, and the left-hand one takes you backwards. The problematic thing to appreciate is that this is not a throttle, you cannot put it on level 5 and pull it lightly to edge forward, it is an on-off switch. If you set it to 5, the rear wheels spin and you set of like a Formula 1 racer. If you mistakenly pull on the left-hand lever the same happens but now in reverse. It isn't difficult, but it is also not entirely intuitive, and so it takes a little getting used to. Diane found a picnic table, and they sat down. I approached and would need to edge in, gently pressing the lever. Not realising that the setting was still high I lurched forward dangerously, stopped, lurched and stopped, lurched again and came to a halt in just the right place and switched the scooter off ready for lunch. I looked up, and my family who were in the path of this bucking bronco ride stared at me open-mouthed. 'What?' I asked.

I arranged with my GP for a wheelchair assessment. My first assessment was conveniently on the first floor at the furthest point down long hospital corridors. With time I was just able to walk that distance, but I wondered how frequently corpses of those who had given up the ghost were cleared away. As I arrived, I was kindly ushered by a small woman who introduced herself as Mary, into her consulting room.

I sat on a tall, sturdy armchair next to her desk. A coffee mug on Mary's desk boasted "World's Best Golfer." A humble mug seems an inadequate way to mark such an achievement, and it needs to up its game. Lesser golfers such as Tiger Woods earned millions and received trophies to fill numerous display cabinets. I decided that it would be better not to ask about her golfing achievements. This would imply interest and my conversational knowledge would falter quickly.

Fortunately, there was no need to make small-talk. Mary had a long list of questions and measurements to get through first, which she completed with warmth and efficiency. We concluded that what I needed was a manual wheelchair that would be made to measure. She asked whether I wanted a self-propelling wheelchair, i.e. one with large back wheels that I could move myself. If I was always going to be pushed, then small wheels are more compact and all that is needed. I hoped that I would be able to push myself, so she suggested that I have a go in one of their chairs. If you have ever watched people dashing around a wheelchair tennis match, you may be surprised to know that propelling a manual wheelchair, even in a straight line isn't as easy as it looks. Turning requires significant force. Once you have started and gained momentum, you need strength to stop. As soon as you introduce any slope, the necessary muscle strength required increases exponentially.

Fortunately, I still had some upper arm strength, so I was able to propel the chair with care on the level. My fingers don't fold conventionally and tend to stick out flat. I had to find the best position to hold my hands so that my fingers didn't act like rattling Spokies, being pushed aside painfully by each turning wheel spoke.

I probably wouldn't be able to propel myself far, but the ability to occasionally wheel myself to a toilet or move to a different view when not being pushed adds a very welcome level of independence.

Mary also measured up a cushion, being comfortable is very important. It would be made of a special foam to help prevent my bum from getting sore after long periods of sitting in the same place.

Mary said that she would send the order immediately, the cushion would arrive in a few days. The chair, however, would be a little later. It would have to come from America. Apparently, we don't make suitable wheelchairs in the UK, this seems amazingly short-sighted of British Industry as in essence, they are a bit of tubular metal with a material seat and wheels. After they arrived in the country, the chair had to be shipped across the country to another centre to check that it meets

British specifications and standards. Apparently, we are happy for Americans to make our wheelchairs, but we don't trust them. I don't know what thorough testing is undertaken, but I suspect that it is probably more likely to be a casual glance followed by "looks OK" than teams of scientists wheeling crash dummies round extreme all-weather test circuits. In about six weeks and when the centre is fully satisfied, the chair would be sent out to me.

True to her word, exactly six weeks later, my smart new wheelchair arrived in a bright greenish-blue colour. The man who delivered my chair showed how the quick release wheels worked and how to adjust the belt. Then he was on his way to the next delivery. I thought that the chair looked quite sporty. Perhaps not that sporty, but as I can only manage to wheel myself a few metres, it is not used for a double backflip or a one-wheeled spin as performed by Aaron "Wheelz" Fotheringham. The nearest that I could get to experiencing Aaron's thrills would be to buy the Wheelie Chair, the Hot Wheels toy he inspired.

Diane has a lot of experience of pushing wheelchairs as she has taught children with all sorts of special needs. She naturally wanted to see how easy it would be for her to manoeuvre. At this point, I discovered that I had released all control. Diane enjoyed demonstrating her ability to tip the chair and balance it on the two rear wheels with just two fingers. I didn't entirely trust Diane's judgement passing through a doorway, and so I gave a significant push on one wheel, resulting in my fingers catching in the spokes, and I learned to trust a little bit more.

A transfer board is the most straightforward invention, the inventor of the wheel would have mocked its simplicity. Yet for many people who use a wheelchair, it is their most essential piece of equipment. In essence, it is a short plank,. My favourite one is about 70cm or so long and less than 1cm thick. The important thing is that one side is polished. If you want to get in or out of a car or onto a chair and you are unable to stand you need beefy carer, a hoist, or if you are healthy enough, you can heave yourself ungracefully across the gap. Trouser pockets or belt straps can always find something to snag onto. A full moon exposure may not be the best beginning of a romantic evening at a local restaurant, and other diners now look nauseously at the succulent rump steak just placed in front of them. If you misjudge things you end up dangerously sinking into the gap and you can quickly end up on the floor and unable to get up. I can assure you that things get very ungraceful at this point, and it becomes tough to regain the feeling of romantic anticipation.

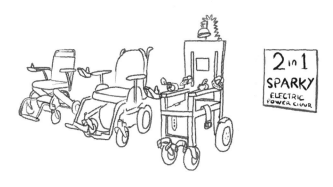

CHAPTER 20

ELECTRIC DREAMS

Mechanical wheelchairs became more widely available at the beginning of the 20th Century. These were an updated version of General Fairfax's chair and powered by hand pedals or pump arms. I watched a YouTube video of a man using a wheelchair made by Gendron Wheel Company of Perrysburg, Ohio. It was a rather beautiful framed contraption with caned seat with a tall back and leg panels. On each side was a hand-cranked chain-driven wheel. The chair was surprisingly mobile and manoeuvrable. The Imperial War Museum in Manchester has one such chair that was issued to an airman who lost his legs in the war. Remarkably he used this chair to propel himself from Lands End to John O'Gr oats.

Mechanically propelled chairs are ideal if you have a lot of upper body strength, if not you need a bit of power. Stanley

Engineering and R A Harding Company manufacturers of self-propelled tricycles recognised this problem and both rival companies developed powered models by adding engines or electric motors. These were substantial machines and suitable for use outside and on roads, but unless you lived in a stately home, they were too big to use inside. In 1947 some brave adventurer crossed the Alps using a petrol-powered Stanley wheelchair called an Argson. I don't know who this was, but I like to think that perhaps it was the legless airman seeking new adventures. Presumably disabled users of these chairs were delighted with the extension to their horizon and newfound independence. I have seen pictures of people racing their Argsons, so they obviously thought that they were a lot of fun.

George Klein was an inventor and a particularly productive one. His contributions included the first system for classifying snow coverage and adding skis to aircraft. Not hugely useful in the UK, but much more so in his snow-covered Canadian homeland. He also designed all-terrain vehicles, a staple gun for use in surgery, the first nuclear reactor outside of the USA and the robotic crane-like Canadarm that deploys and grabs satellites from the Space Shuttle. After the Second World War, many injured veterans returned to Canadian, including John Counsell, a Canadian officer who lost the use of his legs after being shot through the back at Dieppe. John was a fighter, and so started a new battle for more significant veteran support. He was also dissatisfied with his manual wheelchair. This came to the attention of George, who went on to develop a powered chair with a joystick and separate wheel drives enabling a tight turning circle, technologies that are still features of electric wheelchairs today.

One day Tracy and Pascal called round. They, together with Andrew and Ann, have been friends of ours for many years, and we still meet for a meal once a year, now with our families. I knew Tracy before Pascal since he first came to join her from France many years ago. I offered them a drink, I had thoughtfully saved a bottle of Waterloo Beer for Pascal. They had brought pictures of a scooter, and they wondered if it would be of use to me. It was a grand looking machine that had belonged to someone who attended their church but had recently boarded the stair-lift to heaven and so no longer needed it. The family hoped that it would be of use to someone else. It would be ideal to go shopping if we lived a bit closer to the town. Unfortunately, it was too big to put into a car or store in the house, and so regretfully I declined. Hopefully, it found an appreciative new owner.

I decided though that it was time to buy a power chair or a scooter. I looked at portable scooters, and it was self-evident that they were not right for me. To get up, I need to lift all my weight on the scooter arms, which are simply not designed to take this force. We had booked on a cruise, and it was probable that I wouldn't be walking much and I would be dependent on my family to get anywhere onboard ship.

I could have gone for another wheelchair assessment, but this wouldn't solve all my problems. The chairs they offer are ideal, except portability isn't really high on the list of considerations. A power chair would quickly fill my car boot, and many would be too big to fit. Besides, I already have other items, such as a toilet frame to carry. This wouldn't be ideal when going on holiday. Diane and the children are all very forbearing but do insist on somewhere to sit in the car and room to pack a change of underwear or two. Besides power chairs are hefty, most are upwards of 50kg, so I would need some way to get it into the car, possibly a hoist or a ramp, each taking more room. A new car would be an option, but if you have a power chair, you are really looking at something like an adapted van. It seemed each solution led to more problems.

On the internet, I found a folding electric wheelchair that looked great. It was light and compact when folded. Unfortunately, it had not yet arrived in the UK. Due to the folding mechanism, the seat height wasn't adjustable, so it would be a little low for me, but I thought that I could address that with a raised cushion. It was built in China but was available in Australia. I decided to take the risk and order one.

It amazes me how quickly things can arrive on your doorstep from China. These days it is easier than ever to save the world. For only £6.89 I can buy a lovely new plastic recycling bin. This price includes the cost to be flown the 5,000 miles from China. At this price, I can buy a new one every time it gets a bit dirty. To complete the cycle, the discarded bin will be shipped halfway across the world to some country willing to dump it in the sea. From there my dustbin goes on to choke a few playful whales before eventually breaking down into millions of toxic particles, distributed by the currents to the four corners of the ocean, before being filtered out by molluscs and other sea creatures, thereby poisoning the food chain.

Within about a fortnight we received a delivery of a big box. It must have flown over to arrive so quickly, and I felt guilty about how much I had added to my carbon footprint. Why don't we build many great things in the UK any more?

To reduce the worry of running out of power, I also bought a second battery. Most current power chairs use heavy sealed lead-acid batteries, much like a car battery. Weight doesn't seem to factor into their design. My new chair had lithium-ion batteries which are much lighter and still very powerful. With both batteries, I could travel over 20 miles without a recharge.

Electric wheelchairs are simple to use, really simple. The joystick, as George Klein designed, moves the chair in the direction you point it. You can even rotate the chair on the spot, and manoeuvre around shopping aisles. There are two buttons to press one to increase the speed and the other to reduce it. The way it moves feels natural and straight forward, and it is easy to forget that it is a heavy machine.

I saw an old lady scooter user interviewed on TV. She was furious at children and other pedestrians who don't get out of her way. She argued that if she hit someone, it was by definition their fault. I'm not sure that you don't have some responsibility to stop and not leave a trail of maimed toddlers.

Admittedly in the past, I have run over Emily's toes, trying to manoeuvre in a small lift, believe me, she wasn't at all happy. She frequently reminds me of this unfortunate event and tells me that this was only one of numerous occasions which she goes on to list in great detail. I also ran over Diane's toes, but as she once parked a car on my foot, it doesn't count.

There are a few skills that are important to master. I discovered the need to judge the height of a curb. If it were too big, my chair would simply stop with a thump. If I approached at an angle or a bit fast, it would be a big thump, and it wouldn't be hard to become a human catapult. I also discovered the need to set the speed setting to very slow. My chair is powered from the rear wheels, and I found by experience that if I set the things too high and the wheels climbed the curb, the chair would rear up dangerously. Surprised pedestrians would look on in horror as I mount the pavement like a cowboy riding a bucking bronco.

Travelling across a slope is another technique to master. As a family, we once visited Nottingham Castle. As we approached the entrance, my chair had different ideas and decided to take a different route downhill towards the fence. Having just agreed that we would go in, Diane looked on bemused, believing perhaps, I had unrealistically chosen to jump the barrier Steve MacQueen style, rather than pay.

The front wheels of my chair are not powered, and so they will naturally tend to turn to point you downhill. To avoid this, you need to steer a little bit uphill. There is a point where the slope reaches a pitch that even this doesn't work and the chair is only willing to go straight up or down the hill. When a pavement that slopes across its width, the risk is that it will turn involuntarily into the road.

I have a horn button, but this is the most disappointing feature of the chair. The consequence of pressing the impressive button is an electronic squeak with about as much volume as a mouse with laryngitis. There aren't many times when I need a horn, but it would be reassuring to know that I would be able to warn someone of an impending catastrophe. If the conditions were favourable, they might just wonder if they heard someone's phone receiving a text, just before being mown down. There are those times when someone parks their shopping trolley across an aisle, and they take ages to decide which brand of butter to use. When my patience is exhausted, I politely ask if they would mind if I could pass. Unfortunately, they are engrossed in the butter decision, so in a louder voice, I ask "Excuse me please." Still absorbed in the choice between Kerrygold and Anchor, no part of their brain would register my increasingly frenetic pleas. These are the times that I would love a deafening klaxon air horn.

On one hydrotherapy visit, I was using my wheelchair to get to pool from the car park and heard a strange sound which I ignored in the belief that it would go away. A minute later, the strut supporting the front right wheel collapsed almost throwing me from the chair. I regained a sort of balance by sitting back, but the chair wasn't going anywhere. Luckily the physios who accompany us are a muscular group, the type of people who enjoy triathlons, cycling across countries and running up mountains, so they had no trouble sorting me out. My chair was in a mess.

I was pleased to find a local wheelchair repair service and made an appointment to bring it in for their technician to see. Now, this is where it gets a bit technical. I explained to the technician that the flexible unadjusted couplet key's electronically defunct, although I might have used the acronym. He seemed to understand the problem. It transpired that it was a simple fix, and within a day, I was back on the road. If something does break, I am dependant on the goodwill of others. A friend's power chair broke down leaving him stranded on a pavement. Fortunately, a passing motorist realised that there was a problem and kindly offered him and his chair a lift home. It is easy to underestimate how big and bulky power chairs are, so it was very fortunate that this Samaritan was muscular and had a big car. Some insurance companies provide breakdown cover for wheelchairs, but it seems like an opportunity that Green Flag, the RAC and the AA are missing out on. I was once towed home by an AA van, and in a car, it is quite an exciting experience. It would be exhilarating in a wheelchair.

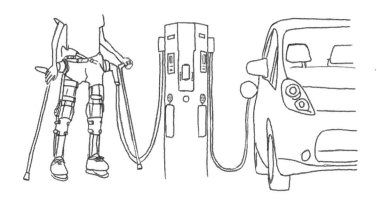

CHAPTER 21

THE WRONG TROUSERS

The idea of exoskeletons is nothing new. Götz von Berlichingen, German mercenary knight, had a reputation as a Robin Hood, protecting peasants from their oppressors. In 1508 he lost his right arm in the Battle of Landshut. Götz was the type of man who said "Lick my arse," actually he was the man who secured his place in history by coining the phrase.

He had over 47 years of experience of being a mercenary and fought in numerous military campaigns and feuds. In 1512 after raiding a group of Nuremberg merchants returning from the great fair at Leipzig and presumably asking them to participate in some bottom slobbering, Emperor Maximilian placed Götz under an Imperial ban. An Imperial Ban was like a medieval red card, and anyone was allowed to rob, injure or kill them without legal consequences until Maximilian was paid a substantial ransom. In 1518 Götz received another ban after demanding payment after kidnapping Philip IV, Count of Waldeck.

During the siege of the city of Landshut, his foes evidently had enough of Götz's dirty-minded rants and shot at him with a cannon. The cannonball missed Götz but hit his sword which flew out of his hand and chopped his forearm off below his elbow. He had a mechanical prosthetic iron replacement arm made. He evidently decided that improvements could be made to the design and a second, more capable prosthetic hand was made able to grip objects such as a shield or a quill. Both arms have survived and are on display in Germany. His new arm enabled him to continue to live his feuding and battling until he retired to his castle in later life. Despite not being very cuddly, his new arm didn't seem to impede his love life. Götz married twice and left three daughters and seven sons.

At about the same time Ambroise Paré, a French army barber-surgeon, was inventing prosthetic devices, including Le Petit Lorrain, "a mechanical hand, operated by catches and springs, worn by a French Army captain in battle." Many of his innovations such a locking knee and suspension harness are used in prosthetics in use today.

In 1890 Nicholas Yagn, a Russian inventor, received a patent for a pneumatically powered exoskeleton to help walking and running. 27 years later Leslie Kelly invented and patented the Pedomotor which had the advantage of being a steam engine mounted on your back pulling on artificial ligaments to power your legs. I would love to wear a steam-powered walking machine, imagine walking into shops and restaurants billowing clouds of steam and smoke. Unfortunately, neither of these devices were successfully manufactured.

In the 1960s came the Hardiman, the first working powered exoskeleton, intended to allow the wearer to lift loads of 1500 pounds with ease. General Electric developed this massive machine inspiring many future sci-fi authors, although they never managed to work out the controls. Every time they started up the Hardiman, it would shake so violently and move so uncontrollably that no one dared to try and wear it.

Exoskeletons are beginning to enable some people who had used wheelchairs to walk again. People with spinal injuries have completed marathons with the help of robotic legs. They are cumbersome, and the technology is still in its infancy, more used for rehabilitation in hospital than everyday use. I was very interested in their possibility and enquired about several products. Things have developed fast over the last couple of years, and one or two exciting products have been launched around the world. As with any new technology, it is at a phase where the prices are exorbitant, and its practical usefulness is likely to be limited. Fortunately, there are some pathfinders, and there will come the point when this reverses, the prices fall, and the technology improves.

I look forward to the day that there is something really usable. I will be lining up to get one. However, I could just attach a small steam engine on my back as a backup power source.

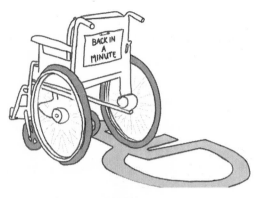

CHAPTER 22

PARKING

I pulled into a disabled parking space outside the supermarket. It was busy, so I had waited for some time for a free space. I picked up my hat and sticks ready to get out. By the time I had got out of the car the next car along had also moved out and a big black new Range Rover pulled next to me.

I try not to judge people because there are many disabilities, like heart conditions that are not visible. Cystic fibrosis is one of those unfair conditions that have a massive impact on the lives of affected young people. I knew a courageous young woman who spent the final years of her life campaigning to build a local Cystic Fibrosis unit, the benefits of which she would never see. Her diet included pretty much everything that we would consider unhealthy, pizza, cream cakes, pork pies but this was necessary to try and maintain her body weight. She would spend weeks and months desperately ill in hospital but looked like she had just come out of a gym.

If you are unable to walk 80m or cannot use a parking meter, you may be entitled to a blue badge. I can't say about the Range Rover driver's difficulties with a parking meter, but her run into the shop gave me reason to suspect that she didn't have significant mobility problems. That and the marathon runners club shirt she was wearing. Oh yes and the sports bag with a tennis racket on her passenger seat. Whatever the reason she had neglected to put out her blue badge.

I went into the shop to do my shopping. The woman was choosing some fruit. On my list were blueberries, but they were placed on a higher shelf out of my reach. It is straightforward to get the wrong initial impression of people, and I asked her if she could please pass me a packet. She had a kind looking face and a kind sounding voice which she used to tell me to kindly piss off.

You may wonder whether blue badge parking abuse is a real problem, surely no one is low enough to intentionally park in a disabled parking space. The past Chancellor of The Exchequer, George Osborne's integrity is beyond question. Admittedly I don't exactly know what the problem is but it is definitely isn't "Would you park in a disable parking space because it was more convenient to get a quick MacDonald's?" as in April 2013 when he was photographed on the front page of the Daily Mirror doing precisely this. George's quote was that he hadn't seen that it was a disabled bay. Perhaps while he was stuffing his face with French fries, he didn't notice the signs, the yellow lines or the prominent wheelchair symbol on that bay or the empty next-door bay.

At a time when he was pushing through welfare reforms that had raised enormous fears amongst the disabled community. George is next in line to inherit the title of Baron of Ballentaylor and Ballylemon, but I think he had already earned another title.

As anyone with a Blue Badge will know. George is not alone. It may be a parent using the disabled space to pick up their child from school, seemingly oblivious that they are there at precisely the same time as disabled parents. Alternatively, it may be someone with a great big car who doesn't want the risk of getting their car scratched. According to the Baywatch Survey by the Disabled Driver's Association in 2017, over 23% of all people parking in blue badge spaces were not entitled to park there. People who feel that in some way the rules don't apply to them.

Presumably thinking why does it matter, it's just a parking space, just move on. A common comment is "No one was using the space." They appear to have a fundamental misunderstanding of the nature of a parking space as you are only able to use parking spaces that no one else is using, that is unless you own a tank or a giant wheeled monster truck.

If you are disabled, the options are fewer, you cannot park down the hill, or on some rough ground, standard spaces are not wide enough to get out of the car or safely unload your wheelchair. It is frustrating to have to wait, but it is more frustrating to have to unsuccessfully return home to try another day.

Sometimes parking is free if you have a blue badge and it is a welcome advantage. Although I don't mind paying, the pay machines can be really frustrating, my sausage fingers find it very difficult to get coins out of my wallet and to put them into the ticket machine. If they use a card reader, the card needs to be pushed right in, and my fingers are not strong enough to pull it out. I have found I can usually extract it with two hands. If not, I have to ask someone for assistance.

Free parking isn't the only advantage. On one shopping visit, the checkout operator started to scan my items and offered to pack them.

"Must be one advantage?" she said "someone packing your bag."

I chuckled, but I didn't want to disillusion her and point out that I can still pack a bag. She was doing a great job.

"That and the parking." she continued

"The bigger spaces help, because I'm useless at parking" I replied. I could have pointed out other reasons that disabled parking is necessary, but I judged that she knew that and so I decided to join in with the direction of the conversation. "and being in a wheelchair, I don't hit my head on low beams..."

Believe me, this is a definite advantage if you are tall, you will know. I am 6'4" standing up or more commonly now, lying down. Many years ago Diane and I were enticed into a little tea room at Bourton-on-the-Water in the Cotswolds, filled with people contentedly munching their way through teacakes, cream teas and cakes. I failed to notice that the beams that gave the room the old world appeal were lower than I was high. Not much lower, perhaps an inch above eye height. I hit the first beam with such force that anyone upstairs would have assumed that the building had been hit by a runaway lorry. The cafe went quiet apart from an audible "Oooooch". Resembling Basil Fawlty, I stood bent double with my head in my hands while behind me Diane gently giggled and gradually the silence started to feel awkward, so people returned to their conversations.

The checkout operator pointed out that wasn't a problem for her, being less than 5' there were few places where beams were that low. I decided not to mention cheaper theatre tickets or priority notification of powercuts in case she was overwhelmed with the enormity of the advantage leading her to sever her own legs.

Blue badge parking spaces are an advantage, but they are also necessary. When I would walk into a shop, being close by was really important, I simply couldn't safely make it across a supermarket car park. Now that I use a wheelchair, being close by isn't so important, but it needs space to unload the chair, the reason for the hatched areas. There have been times when there are no blue badge spaces, and I have been forced to park elsewhere. It becomes really awkward and sometimes perilous for anyone trying to unload my chair.

CHAPTER 23

INACCESSIBLE PLACES

You may be shocked, and I've never admitted this before, but I feel empathy with the most malevolent beings in the Universe. You may not like Daleks, but you have to admire their sheer ability to bounce back and their limitless ambition. Unfortunately, the environment on earth is quite disabling. Their quest to invade and conquer is tough when access is blocked by some moron who has parked in front of a dropped curve. At least they have an exterminate option.

Daleks may have a happier time in Ireland. If you block a pavement there, you may find that someone from the Makewayday disabled access campaign has attached a sticker printed with "Hey, this blocks my way" and posted a picture of it on Twitter or Facebook.

In recent times it seems that Daleks have had a handy levitate upgrade, presumably part of a package including gesticulate, defenestrate and redecorate. This adaptation has helped where access ramps, lifts or access to work grants were unavailable. Perhaps they would be kind enough to share the technology with wheelchair users. It would do wonders for their tarnished reputation.

In 1964, just after the first episode of Dr Who when Daleks invaded England, a disabled architect Selwyn Goldsmith, went to live in Norwich. He spent his time interviewing people with disabilities and discovered that they were restricted where they could go because there were no accessible public toilets. Restaurants, local shops, and churches and other buildings that reflected ordinary lives were equally inaccessible. Architects had given no thought to designing buildings with disabled people in mind.

They were making buildings which placed barriers in the way of disabled people who wanted to use them. He called this "architectural disability". He also pointed out that removing these barriers didn't just help people in wheelchairs or mobility problems but also blind and deaf people, or anyone who had difficulty negotiating buildings.

His work resulted in England's first unisex, disabled-access public toilet (on Castle Hill in Norwich). He also introduced the innovation of 15 ramped kerbs around the city. He produced guidance for other architects called "Designing for the Disabled" so that many of his ideas are now standard good practice around the world.

The Purple Pound, the collective spending power of disabled people, is something that few businesses and services have fully woken up to. Some seven million people of working age have a disability in the UK, which all adds up to an awful lot of spending power. In fact about £249billion worth, so why wouldn't you want to do everything to attract disabled people to spend their money with you. If this isn't enough of an incentive, the law requires that you make reasonable adjustments to allow access. But what is reasonable? The short answer is, it depends. If you own an old working windmill that opens to the public, your options may be limited. Sometimes there are no practical ways to make changes to an old building, but if you own a bank with a step into the front door, there are lots of things you could do. Big organisations have more resources available to them to make changes.

Occasionally I see shops with a bell outside underneath a disabled sign. We recently went to Edinburgh to watch my son acting in the Fringe. We had arrived on the tram, and it was raining. I knew that Jenners, Scotland's oldest department store, was nearby and it seemed like an excellent place to find some shelter and a cafe. Unfortunately, all the entrances have steps. The side entrance is probably the grandest and at in a prominent position is a bell-button and sign. We pressed it expecting that somewhere in a deep basement a bell would be ringing away unnoticed. We were wrong, and within seconds a smartly dressed doorman appeared with a portable ramp in hand. This was laid out and dripping wet we were able to climb into the beautiful atrium, and from there we went up to the cafe in the cramped lift.

When we left the shop the exit, there was a different doorman who didn't appear as familiar with the ramp. The entrance in on a sloping street, so at one end there are three steps and at the other four. This makes a considerable difference to the steepness of the ramps. The new doorman chose to put the ramp over the four steps. Perhaps I should have said something, but fearlessly I drove onto the top. Suddenly the chair accelerated at a rate that I hadn't previously experienced, and I rushed headlong down the ramp, bumping off the bottom, narrowly missing a few unsuspecting pedestrians, breaking just before I flew off the curb into the road.

Now for another admission, I don't enjoy clothes shopping with my wife. Throughout human history, many millions of hours have been miserably spent by husbands following their wives from shop to shop and waiting as their wives add more clothes to the overladen basket they are carrying. Well if that is the stereotype, we certainly don't conform. I quite like shopping, but my wife gets bored with shopping quickly, very quickly. In fact, so fast that there have been occasions when we haven't made it through the doors of the shop before she decides to go home and buy something online instead. On rare occasions, even Diane decides that we need to go and buy some clothes, and so we take a trip to a local shopping centre.

I am tall, about 194cm, but in a wheelchair, not so tall. I now appreciate the advantage of being able to see above the racks and rails across a shop floor. Even in the biggest shops, it wouldn't take long to find my bearings or find Diane. In a wheelchair, it is a different, smaller world. Suddenly all I can see is the row of clothes in front and to the side of me. The piles and racks of clothes are now walls to a maze. However, accessibly designed the shop is, the fittings are movable, and managers like to add shelves to sell more stock. The space between the clothes rails isn't always wide enough to fit a wheelchair. Sometimes, like the entrance to Narnia, I have to push through lines of coats. Other directions are barred by the feet mannequins, the bases of displays narrowing the pathway, pushchairs and bags of shopping. Each time I turn a corner I am eye to crotch with browsing people.

On a recent shopping trip, I noticed that on one main street just outside of the shopping centre, many of the shops had a step into the entrance. The only two shops I could access were a bridal shop and a betting shop, neither of which featured on my shopping list. I wouldn't be able to get through the door of the nail salon, the vaping shop, hair studios, fish and chip shop, clothes shops, most of the estate agents, some cafes and the pub. I had no intention of going into any of these shops, but the fish and chips did smell good and being unobtainable, perhaps all the more so.

My local High Street is a little better, and in places, the pavement has been gently raised. This means that I can access some small shops, like an old fashioned sweet shop. As it is always full of children and their parents, getting out would be a challenge and would involve asking everyone shuffle round.

To be fair, most of the High Street shops are accessible. I couldn't get into the opticians, but the eye tests are done upstairs so I can understand that the costs to adapt the premises wouldn't be proportionate for such a small business.

I also couldn't access HSBC Bank, Nat West Bank and Barclay's Bank. HSBC had a bell with a wheelchair symbol outside, but there were five or six steps into the bank. I've not seen a portable ramp that would reach that high, so I would have been interested in seeing how they would have responded. Nat West had fewer steps but no bell. Both banks were old buildings, and it would have been a costly job to make them accessible, but there were lots that they could have done. In their defence, they did make them equally accessible for everyone, or rather equally inaccessible, as they closed the branches. Now, whether or not you are disabled, you have to go nine miles to the nearest accessible branch.

One bank still has a branch. I wouldn't want to name the bank, but there is a certain irony that it is the only one of the big four banks that rhymes with disabled parking bays. On their website, they say that this branch is wheelchair accessible and so I phoned the branch to make sure. Actually, I phoned the virtual branch in a call centre somewhere in the world as unfortunately, it has been many years since you can actually phone someone who has ever visited the actual branch you want to know about. They told me that the branch was "absolutely, totally accessible", by which I think he meant that he had seen the wheelchair symbol on their website. On the window, there is also a tiny sign that says the branch is accessible to all. Unfortunately, it doesn't say how you are meant to negotiate the big step in the entrance. Maybe I should shout "Could someone help me" through the doorway, or perhaps there is another entrance at the rear, they don't say. I felt a bit self-conscious about shouting, and although I have lived here a long time, I have never ventured around the dingy back entrances.

I'm left wondering how on earth is this accessible. If you have a strapping carer and a manual wheelchair, it may be possible to use this branch. If you are unable to climb a step, use an electric wheelchair, or you are a pre-upgrade Dalek, then the step in the entrance is an impenetrable blockade. The small independent sweet shop down the road has addressed a similar problem without difficulty, yet this multinational bank with assets of over £1 trillion has not been able to raise the entrance a few inches or even provide any suitable information about how to get in.

Steps are not the only predicament people in wheelchairs face. If you stop at Killington Lake service station on the M6 and you use a wheelchair, you will encounter the problem of corridors. There is a disabled toilet, but for some reason, they have located it at the end of a corridor shared with a shower room. To find out if there is anyone in the toilet, you need to venture down the hallway past the shower room. If it is occupied, then you have to reverse back down as there will be no room to pass. Now add the complication of a hiker waiting in the corridor for the shower room, who has taken the opportunity to empty his rucksack to find his towel.

Worse still is our local theatre at Lichfield. It is a lovely little theatre, and we have enjoyed some first-class productions. The architect, however, was an idiot. There are half floors so wheelchair users have no option but to use the lift. Unfortunately, the lift is down a small corridor with a 90° turn at the end, so you have to go down and manoeuvre the chair round to press the call button. If anyone is coming out of the lift, you have to reverse the process. At the start and end of the play, everyone wants to use the lift at the same time.

Diane and I went to the funeral of a friend, we each knew her but separately. Diane worked with her, but she had been a friend of mine during my teenage years. One day she felt dizzy. Within a couple of weeks, doctors discovered that she had an inoperable brain tumour and within six months she was dead. Before the funeral, we needed to know whether I would be able to get into the church.

Little things bug me. The Church of England website called "A Church Near You" has a pleasingly simple search page and there are just two bits of information to fill in. The second box asks for your location, which is sensible. The first box asks for a tag and helpfully offers two suggestions "choir or disabled access". Brilliant, couldn't be easier, and it even provides disabled access as an option. But there is a problem. As you start typing d...i... a list of 8 available tags appears including anything including the letters di "Listed buildings, Addiction Services...Weddings". Type d...i...s... and the only option for a tag is "Discipleship Course". At this point, I am not sure that I would qualify for this, in addition to my atheist beliefs, I have some very unchristian thoughts. Despite suggesting disabled access as a term to search, no one has set this up as a tag. I try several options and find that you have to type "Ramped Access, Accessible Toilet or Accessible Car Parking".

I wonder what Jesus thinks about this. All those miracles curing the lame and the blind and some dickhead screws up the website. Perhaps the reason cripples aren't miraculously cured these days is that they can't find the accessible churches.

According to the website, the church apparently had an accessible toilet so you would imagine it had ramped access. It always helps to have all the information on the website, even if it seems obvious. I have learned that nothing can be taken for granted so, I phoned the vicar to make sure. In fact, the church was ideal, and we found a place to park me next to a pew where Diane sat.

CHAPTER 24

RAMPS

If you were standing on the top of Masada almost 2000 years ago, you would have known how brilliant the Romans were at building access ramps. Herod the Great built two fortified palaces on the top of Masada. According to the Bible, Herod ordered the massacre of innocents, the execution of all young male children under two in the vicinity of Bethlehem. He also killed three of his sons, his mother in law, his second wife and to make sure people really missed him when he died he imprisoned the most prominent citizens with the order that they would be executed after he died. I suspect he was called Herod the Murdering Bastard by more than a few people. The palaces were a place where humble Herod could put his feet up in comfort and safety after some busy murdering and slaughtering while his revolting subjects and armies squabbled away beneath him.

Masada was really impregnable, as a young man I climbed with a friend up the narrow path cut into the sheer slopes to the only entry point and we stayed the night (you are really not allowed to do this) to watch the sunrise over the Dead Sea. It is one of the most spectacular views in the world, so Herod must have enjoyed his summer breaks there.

A little time after Herod, Masada became the stronghold home of a group of warring Jewish rebels called the Sicarii. Masada was completely inaccessible. This really got under the skin of Lucius, the Roman Governor of Judea, so he decided to build a 114m high access ramp to the summit, and with the help of a few thousand slaves, it was completed in a couple of months. The purpose of the access ramp wasn't so much for wheelchairs and soldiers with mobility problems as for an enormous siege tower, battering ram and hoards of bloodthirsty legionaries. The Sicarii had been watching the ramp inevitably progressing to their walls and decided that rather than wait for a horrible death on the end of a Roman sword, they would get it over with and kill themselves. When the Romans broke through the walls, there were just two women and five children alive.

The Roman ramp is still there, but a lot of it had eroded away over the past 2,000 years, so unsurprisingly Masada is still about as inaccessible as it gets for anyone in a wheelchair.

OK, let's do a small thought experiment. Imagine some stairs, or better still, stand at the bottom of a flight as this really helps to visualise the next stage. Now picture a long sheet of plywood and lay this down on the stairs. Remember this is only a thought experiment, no need to go out to the shed. Now imagine a chair, a good sturdy wooden dining chair with arms and place this on the plywood about halfway up the stairs facing upwards. It should be reasonably clear by now why this is only a thought experiment. Would you be happy to sit on the chair? Would it be better if the chair was facing downwards? Hold on, we are not there yet. Now imagine that you do the same experiment on a really long flight of steps, perhaps the sort you might get at a railway or tube station, or if you are really adventurous, the type you see when you are on holiday and the stairs, together with the number of steps, are mentioned in the guidebook. Marble would be a suitable material to make these steps as it is hard and slippy. Finally, bolt rollerskates to the feet of the chair and repeat. In case you decided to try this for real I would like to point out that I did say this is a thought experiment! I suspect that you will have come to the conclusion that attempting this would be tantamount to committing suicide. Even if your name is Eddie the Eagle, you will have probably concluded that there are health and safety implications and attempting it would be unwise without precautions including a helmet, protective clothes and lots of padding.

If you want to be able to propel yourself in a wheelchair up a ramp, the maximum recommended gradient for a rise of one step would be the length of 10 steps. If you are muscular or have a power chair, you could possibly manage a gradient twice that, but things have already got scary. In road terms, this is a steep 20% hill. This is the same gradient as Kirkstone Pass in Cumbria aptly known as 'The Struggle'.

There are a few contenders for Britain's steepest road but amongst these is Hardknott Pass in Cumbria. At 1 in 3 (33%) it is not for the faint-hearted, I know from experience, in a Citroen 2CV. Quite an achievement for this impressive little French workhorse of a car but not something that I would recommend or repeat.

The steepest street in the World is Baldwin Street in Dunedin, New Zealand. It is a residential street, but you would really have to like hills to live on this 1 in 2.86 (38%). I doubt many of the residents use bicycles. Now imagine doing this in a wheelchair.

This is self evidently madness, so WTF (pardon my textspeak) are there wheelchair access ramps that are as steep as a flight of steps. You would need to be superhuman to use them. There are not just one or two, but hundreds of them. If you don't believe me go to Google images and type in something like 'wheelchair ramps from hell'. Imagine propelling yourself up a ramp like this. I have seen a picture where this is being attempted with the help of two burly assistants but with extreme difficulty.

Many examples of really scary ramps are in remote places, the old soviet block seems to have its fair share. My first experience of an impossible ramp was into a hotel in Norway, two metal gutters bolted to a flight of steps at the entrance to a restaurant, needless to say, we didn't attempt it. When building these ramps I like to think that at least someone had the right intention along the way, but really, what were they thinking of.

The UK isn't immune from bad ramps, but for the most part, the problem is more likely to be that there is no ramp. In the UK one-fifth of shops are inaccessible in a wheelchair. Most disabled people have experienced visiting somewhere that should be accessible but that they weren't able to access.

The steepness of ramps isn't the only brainless examples you can find. It is easy to find examples that have fallen a bit short, so the builder has added a few steps at the end.

There are even examples where the plans obviously hadn't accounted for a tree or lamppost, so they just built the ramp leaving an impassable obstacle in the middle.

CHAPTER 25

THE GOOD, THE BAD & THE UGLY

The Good

The town I live in is proud of its canal and claims to be "the Canal Town". This seems to lack a basic understanding of the purpose of canals. Like telephones, you need more than one to be of any use, and there are many other towns with canals. It isn't as if there are lots of canals in the town, just one, although there are a couple of attractive old boatyards. If you have been to Venice, the City of Canals, you will find my town a little disappointing. The canal doesn't even flow down the main street. You could just as well call it, Road Town, Charity Shop Town.

It seems that locally Councils love by-lines. I can understand that it gives someone a sense of having done something significant. If I had given a town a by-line, my children would know about it, my family would know about it, I would make sure I was pictured next to the sign, in local papers, and the picture would be copied on every Christmas circular. Whenever I could I would make a detour just to drive past to point out that I was the person responsible for the sign "Welcome to Sellafield, Britain's Chernobyl" or "Welcome to Dudley, Everything a Pound."

Cheadle, a small Staffordshire town, has a mysterious by-line on its town signs "Welcome to Cheadle, Discover the Secret", I wonder which big secret they are referring to. In a small town, there are bound to be some be dark secrets. Cheadle's parish priest was jailed for 22 years when a history of sexual abuse was uncovered at the now-closed Cotton College. While open honesty is admirable, surely the council could highlight some more positive aspects of the town.

Wolverhampton is the site of many industries such as Jaguar Cars, Chubb Locks and until recently Goodyear tyres. Its city signs state that they are "Proud to be the World's leading cask ale brewer" and it is true that Wolverhampton is the headquarters of Marston's Brewery. But in my mind, (therefore I admit the analysis may be flawed) Burton upon Trent has much more justification for putting brewing on their signs as for centuries it has been the primary industry of the town. Even today there are eight breweries. Burton could have had a sign "If you've gone for a Burton, you have arrived." It would be a significant boost to the funeral businesses in the town, but obviously no one in their creative department thought of that. Instead, Burton went for the tagline "Gateway to the National

Forest." This is an essential message as less than a quarter of the National Forest is woodland, and without the signs, you might not be aware that you are driving through it.

Enterprising Crewe has seen the opportunity to sell out its by-lines, and so there are several different versions of the "Welcome to Crewe" signs. Who wouldn't want to visit Crewe with signs like "Home of Ice Cream Vans", "Home of Bentley Motors", "Home of South Cheshire College, Inspire, Believe, Achieve" and if you like your morning cereal "Home of the Mornflake." More enigmatically they also have a tagline "Please Support the Crewe Pledge" with a picture of a strange three-fingered salute. You probably have to be a Mason and live in Crewe to understand this. I have no affection for Crewe, having waited for many hours at Crewe station. I would suggest turning the signs round and add the tagline "You have escaped this God-forsaken place."

Stafford Council has the by-line "The Knot Unites" Unfortunately the Staffordshire knot uses a single rope, so the image doesn't quite work, and if you are even mildly dyslexic the motto reads "The Knot Unties."

Staffordshire's tag line is "The Creative County". It seems an irony that this is the best its creative department could do. Sorry, other counties you are obviously not as creative as we are. We make big diggers, have creative ways of saving your money at the Britannia Building Society based in Leek or even more creative ways taking your cash with Bet 365, one of the biggest online betting companies. Some people have created ways of scaring you half to death at Alton Towers theme park, and in Stoke, they still make a few teapots and a bit of crockery. The real evidence of Staffordshire's creativity can be found on the back pages of colour supplements and magazines. Only from Staffordshire can you buy gifts like the Illuminated 3D John Wayne Cuckoo Clock. Actually cuckoo is a bit of a misnomer as there is no bird, at the top of every hour, the barn doors open, and John's horse Dollar appears to the sound of galloping hooves. Or you can buy a 'Jewel Of Nature' Robin Musical Egg, an opening Fabergé-style egg, that hides a Euro-friendly Robin tweeting away 'Ode To Joy'. These and many other apparently hallucinogen inspired gifts are clear evidence that Staffordshire really does excel as the creative county and in the best possible taste.

Just outside my home town is Meaford Hall. Its onetime owner Craig had a lavish lifestyle, that included two helicopters, gym, sauna, indoor swimming pool, a Bentley, a Ferrari and many other supercars. Unfortunately for Craig, the HMRC discovered that he had amassed £138 million through a little fraudulent chicanery and creative accounting and his wealth was gained through the proceeds of a mobile phone VAT scam. So while Craig's criminal creativity is not in doubt, he ended up with a 12-year prison sentence and a massive bill from the taxman.

There are many thriving creative businesses in Staffordshire and some welcome revivals of the traditional handcrafted potteries. There are also many creative businesses in Cheshire or Shropshire or in any other county. Do creative people from across the country uproot and migrate to the hub of creativity in Staffordshire? Perhaps they do.

Now the tagline that might surprise you is Chester, "The most accessible city in Europe". It was the first British city to win this award since its inception seven years ago. After all, it is an ancient city famed for its two miles of Roman town walls and Tudor style rows with covered walkways to shops on two levels and yet with a commitment over the years. Chester rightfully is attracting more than its share of the purple pound.

The Bad

Of course, there are villains amongst the disabled community. Alan Moore shuffled one step ahead of the police for three years. Armed with only a walking stick, a fake gun and a disabled parking badge he would limp into a bank, brandishing the replica gun to rob cashiers of thousands of pounds.

Meanwhile, his registered carer, brother Barry, kept the getaway car engine running outside. He could park on double yellow lines right outside the bank thanks to his Blue Badge. Cumbria Police said, "Alan was the most unlikely person to have committed armed robbery -- he just did not fit the image most people have of a bank robber."

Another man who used a wheelchair was arrested in Dublin when he attempted to rob a bank with a samurai sword. The Dublin Gardi stated that it was the first time that the Gardi had to deal with an attempted bank robbery by someone in a wheelchair, but not the first time they have seen attempted thefts by a disabled person.

Perhaps the step into the local Barclays branch is a cunning deterrent for the likes of Alan More and the Irish wheelchair bank robber. However, after these stories, you may be surprised to hear that research shows that most bank robberies are done by people who are not in wheelchairs. I say research, I just made it up, but I would be shocked if someone proved me wrong. I would love to see that information. Most of the remainder of the disabled community have led a relatively blame-free life.

The Ugly

In the early 1700s, you wouldn't want to go to town if you were disabled. In all likelihood, your local town wasn't very accessible, but it didn't really matter anyway as you wouldn't have received a friendly welcome. This was the beginning of the age of enlightenment and John Locke, English philosopher, physician and "The Father of Liberalism" had already written 20 years before the start of the century "the state of nature as a condition in which humans are rational and follow natural law, in which all men are born equal and with the right to life, liberty and property." (you probably recognise this as the idea that forms the basis of the American Constitution) So you would think that disabled people would be enjoying their equality and liberty. However, hypocrisies that seem so obvious now perhaps were not so then. Although John Locke's writings criticised slavery, he didn't see the hypocrisy that he was a considerable investor in the English slave trade through the Royal African Company.

In Victorian Britain, the only option for survival for many people with disabilities was begging. Unsightly beggars were kept off the streets and saving citizens from the discomfort of witnessing mutilated, deformed and disabled people begging by the opening of poor houses. They were viewed as worthy poor but effectively incarcerated and given the most rudimentary care.

In the last part of the 19th century, eugenicists argued using false science, that people with impairments, and particularly congenital conditions, would weaken the human gene pool. So increasingly, disabled people were shut away in single-sex institutions for life, or sterilised, and thus the separation in the lives of able and disabled people grew.

In the USA they were perhaps more direct. Many cities and states passed legislation aimed at removing "unsightly" people from the streets to address the growing number of destitute miners and maimed Civil War veterans. The first recorded ugly law arrest was of Martin Oates, an injured Civil War Veteran in San Francisco, California in July 1867. In 1881 Chicago passed an ordinance that read as follows:

"Any person who is diseased, maimed, mutilated, or in any way deformed, so as to be an unsightly or disgusting object, or an improper person to be allowed in or on the streets, highways, thoroughfares, or public places in the city, shall not therein or thereon expose himself to public view, under the penalty of a fine of $1 for each offence"

This, the last remaining US ugly law, was only repealed in 1974. However, in the same year, Nebraska arrested a person with a scarred face for violating its unsightly beggar ordinance, even though the law in that state had been repealed in 1967.

Fortunately, the town I live in doesn't have any ugly laws, and despite being a bit diseased and maimed, I haven't committed any major crimes, and so for many years, the town authorities have allowed me to live a quiet and contented life.

CHAPTER 26

BOGGY PROBLEMS

Your local antique shop would be less than impressed if you defecated on their 18th century French commode as it is likely to discourage other customers from browsing. To be fair, your local shop selling mobility and care aids would generally insist that you buy one of their commodes and take it home before your first test drive.

In 18th century France, a commode was a chest of draws raised on legs. Not just any old chest of draws, but a luxurious ornately decorated, bow fronted, beautiful ebony cabinet with ormolu drawer pulls, raised on short legs and topped with a marble slab.

In Tudor England, if you were posh or infirm, you might have a piece of furniture called a close stool, a lidded box containing a chamber pot. Once you had completed your business, a poor servant would empty the container and clean up.

The king's servant was called the Groom of the Stool and was responsible for assisting the king in his excretion while maintaining a royal decorum over the proceedings. Surprisingly this was a sought after job, and the Groom of the Stool title was generally bestowed on the sons of noblemen, almost literally arse-licking their way into the king's inner circle. There was probably a better way to phrase that.

England's famous cabinet maker, Thomas Sheraton, designed a closed stool with false draws that had the appearance of a small commode. In the middle of the night, you could pull out the bottom section relieve yourself and discretely push it away for a servant to deal with in the morning. Obviously, there would be trouble if you had too much to drink and confused this with your wife's knicker drawer.

From this time the term commode was used as a euphemism for a toilet, hidden in a piece of furniture used primarily by the elderly and infirm.

I have had a commode when I have been confined to bed. These days they have dispensed to disguise its purpose with any attempt of aesthetic beauty. They are generally made from tubular steel and purely functional style. It does feel undignified, being in a room other than a bathroom or toilet, and knowing that someone has to clean up after you, but there are worse things.

Toilets may not be the most agreeable topic, but disabled public toilets are one thing that makes life a more even playing field. Fortunately, there are lots of places with well-designed toilets. Even in busy areas like motorway services and supermarkets, it is often possible to find proper, usable toilets, because of proper management and sometimes the use of Radar keys or a managed key system. Unfortunately, though this is not universal, it amazes me how much mess some people can make and how often there is a broken toilet seat. As with all toilets, there are places where they are fifthly, and some are absolutely gut-wrenchingly disgusting.

Disabled public toilets are principally designed for people in wheelchairs who can transfer onto the toilet; as such they don't meet everyone's needs. If you are unable to transfer you need a hoist, fortunately, there are now a small but growing number of places with hoists. Changing places lists a little over 1000 in England. That sounds like quite a lot, but they are still spread relatively thinly across the country, imagine if there were only 1000 toilets that you could use. Visit Kings Lynne, and there are none. Your nearest option is Peterborough 35 miles away, so cross your legs.

I have difficulty getting out of a chair and would be unable to get off a toilet without a raised seat. It is usual to see helpful folding side rails, but I have yet to see a toilet in a public location where a raised seat is available. For obvious reasons, this is a more significant issue for women. One option is to lug around your own portable seat. Grab rails are a big help, but sometimes they are put in the strangest places that leave you pondering what on earth do some people do in toilets that need a grab rail 30cm above the floor.

Some builders who install disabled lavatories obviously have never tried using the toilet with a wheelchair, or they would have noticed that they haven't left enough room to turn round or transfer to the toilet.

Now, when it comes to door locks, they can be most frustrating. Good door locks use a big leaver which my weak hands can easily close. Often though a standard door lock is used. My pathetic fingers simply don't have the strength to grip and turn the mechanism. I try, but they just slip off. With time and experimentation, I can find a way to clasp the knob between my two weak hands.

I have discovered a biological phenomena. When you enter a toilet, your mind somehow triggers a mental timer. It starts the moment that the door opens. The fumbling over the door lock has already used up valuable time, and things have already begun to feel uncomfortable, the timer is counting down. Next, it takes a while to stand up and steady myself against the grab rails and lift the seat. By this point, the timer has finished and in my head alarm bells are ringing. Like a cork plugging a leak in the Hoover Dam, it is inevitably going to fail, and catastrophe is imminent, yet I have still got everything done up. Manipulating the zip on my flies is an even more difficult problem. Summoning all my willpower I imagine holding in the cork, but it is futile, the cork has started to move. I change tack, and everything comes down. Disaster isn't going to be pleasant, but like a good suspense movie at the very last moment, everything is pointing in the right direction. Blissful relief.

Often there is a small sink to make additional room. This is a sensible compromise; however, it is vital to take care with lever taps, or you will get an unwelcome shower. When you have dried your hands with paper towels, many toilets helpfully provide a pedal bin. I always wonder which was the first organisation to put together a management group to look at their disabled toilet facilities and after hours of meeting, debates and arguments decided that it was a good idea to put a pedal bin in a toilet specifically designed for people who have little or no power in their feet. The worst offenders are hospitals who have exceptionally robust metal pedal bins with a heavy metal recessed lid cannot be opened without elephantine force.

I have used a toilet with a brilliant rising seat. It also had an incredible cleaning system with an inherent problem if you are standing up to use the toilet. I found this out the hard way. When I flushed what I expected didn't happen. Instead, a robotic metal rod appears from under the rim. It mesmerisingly moved to the centre of the bowl, and I suddenly discovered the purpose. The rod emits a powerful spray is designed to clean your under regions. Without a bum seal, however, the toilet becomes an impromptu shower. The power of the spray is sufficient to ricochet off the ceiling. It is accurately angled so that almost all of the water ended up over me and within a couple of seconds, a remarkable amount of water came out. In effect I had, I had just had a shower with my clothes on. It was at that point that I noticed the big sign that explains that you need to raise the seat a little to avoid being soaked.

I dried myself off with paper towels and sheepishly opened the door, hoping that no-one was waiting outside. Months later, I was waiting outside as the door opened and the man who came out had obviously shared the same experience. With a smug feeling, I sympathised with him.

A grim reality is that even with a raised toilet and support bars, I sit down very heavily and I break a lot of toilet seats. I can assure you that a cracked toilet seat can painfully pinch and grip a particularly sensitive piece of skin, so it is very advisable to replace it as soon as possible.

Searching online for a replacement, I came across a Pro Luxury Toilet seat. I'm not sure what makes a luxury toilet seat, but I certainly had no idea that sitting on the toilet could be a profession. You can also buy a Pro fluffy toilet seat cover. I assume that if you sit on the toilet professionally, you need something to keep your bum warm. If you can't get to a toilet you can buy a Pro Commode Chair. I also found a Pro Reaching Grab Sticks and Pro Men's Incontinence Underwear, so it appears that picking things up and wetting yourself are little known but noble professions. Perhaps there is a Guild of Incontinent Men, whose worshipful masters proudly dress in ceremonial golden trousers. I should find out about membership as I'm sure that it won't be too long before I am eligible for membership. The Groom of the Stool would be delighted to know that the tools of his profession, Pro Personal Wipes can now be purchased online. Pro seems to be a current favourite buzz word amongst marketing executives. Television advertisements encourage you to brush your teeth like a pro. Are there really professional teeth brushers or are they highlighting excellent dental hygiene habits of courtesans?

TORTURE CHAMBER

UNSUITABLE FOR

WHEELCHAIR USERS

CHAPTER 27

THE GETAWAY

One of the memories of my childhood, as well as the childhood of our children, was singing in the car. Without the distraction, our children would resort to making up jingles for every business sign we passed, and I mean every sign.

"Visit Harvey Jones doo doo, we sell cars, not phones doo doo."

"Take your cow to Hughes the Butcher, he'll chop her up and then we'll cook her."

There wasn't a business that couldn't inspire a jingle, and if there were no signs, they would make worse jingles.

"Can we stop really quick, or I think I will be sick."

To take their mind off things, we would invent and play games, tell stories and sing songs. One of my favourite car songs, The Hippopotamus song, written by Flanders and

Swann expounded the benefits of glorious mud in enticing a partner.

Michael Flanders and Donald Swann were a very successful British 1950s musical comedy duo who performed their songs, interspersed with comic monologues. Unusually for the time, Michael performed in a wheelchair after contracting polio when he was a young man.

Throughout his career Michael campaigned for better access to theatres for people with disabilities. After his death in 1975, his wife Claudia continued to promote the cause of better transport and more accessible holidays.

We enjoy going to country houses and exploring the buildings and gardens. One day we visited a nearby stately home. We have been there many times to walk in the acres of grounds and woods, as well as picnic in the gardens or have tea in the coffee shop. This time we decided to look round the museum and house. The ticket office was some way from the house and the rough ground not ideal for a wheelchair, so I transferred to one of their scooters. We arrived at the house and had to transfer into one of their rickety-looking manual wheelchairs. We wandered around the house and then through the museum. At one point the museum route led up a flight of stairs and so while Diane, Daniel and Emily went with the rest of the group to see the exhibits upstairs I was taken by one of the volunteers to a small hallway where the stairs descended back to my level. As I waited, the fire alarm went off. The group upstairs were directed out of a fire escape route. Unfortunately, this was not past me. Diane assumed that I was being escorted out separately. In reality, I was in the hallway. I was hopeful that it was a false alarm or an exercise because I was a bit stuck in the hallway. As everyone gathered outside Diane realised that I wasn't there and so shortly afterwards I was liberated by Diane and a small search party. Outside we were told that the museum would be closed for the rest of the day. We never found out if there was a fire, but the museum is still there.

Having a few hours to spare in Oxford, I decided to visit the Ashmolean Museum. In 1605 Guy Fawkes was hiding under the Houses of Parliament waiting with his lantern to ignite barrels of gunpowder and blow away the King and Parliament. Guy was discovered and amongst his captors was Robert Morley who wisely and successfully, struggled to take Guy's lantern from his hand to keep it away from the trail of gunpowder. Robert kept the lamp and carefully looked after it as a souvenir, and so it fared much better than Guy who was tortured and hanged, and his body was quartered and sent to "the four corners of the Kingdom" to deter other would-be traitors. Robert's brother donated the lantern to the Ashmolean where it is displayed today. A direct connection with an event that could have changed the course of history. In another case is a beautiful gold and enamelled pointer that was ploughed up in a field in 1693 with the inscription 'Alfred ordered me to be made'. The Alfred is Alfred the Great who reigned between 871 and 899AD and is famous for burning the cakes.

Further on is a reliquary casket made to house the remains of St Thomas Becket after he fatally fell out with his friend

Henry II. Around another corner is a Stradivari violin called the "Messiah Violin."

They have one artefact, a majolica bowl, that should be dedicated to the person who planned the signage for the toilets. The sign for the toilets takes you down a hallway and to the top of a set of stairs. At the top of the stairs is a sign with a man, woman and a wheelchair and an arrow pointing down the stairs. In the movie The Italian Job, Minis are chased down flights of Rome's steps, but it isn't something I would advise copying in a wheelchair. It is possible to get to the toilets using the lift on the far side of the building, so whoever decided on this sign is utterly deserving of this dedication.

The bowl was made by Francesco Urbini sometime between 1530 and 1540. The interior is painted with a head made up from of interlaced penises and carries the Italian inscription that roughly translates as "dickhead".

There is something that excites me about staying in a hotel, somewhere new and the possibility of an adventure. More often than not the room is disappointingly small and uncomfortable, but that doesn't diminish the excitement of tussling suitcases up flights of steps, to count down the room numbers to find yours, putting the card in the door lock, turning the door handle and repeating the process several times as nothing happens, and until on the point of returning to the reception, Diane decides she should try, and it opens the first time to reveal your room for the night.

Inside we find that there is nowhere to fit the suitcases in the room, so we fill the tiny kettle open a mound of various sugar, milk, coffee and biscuit packets to make a flavourless cup of coffee, then sit on the end of the bed and try to find the one working channel on the television.

I still feel the same excitement although now it is Diane panting through the door with the suitcases and the immense mound of coffee debris with the mangled attempts with my sausage fingers and teeth before Diane took over. The excitement is accentuated simply because we have got there.

There was a time when I would happily arrive in a new country and look for somewhere to stay. Diane liked a little more certainty so that she wouldn't end up sleeping on the back seat of the car and so marriage meant a bit more forethought and booking a bed. I have always liked the unusual and would book accommodation in a windmill, or a lighthouse. I once booked a room in a spooky old hunting lodge in the Cotswolds once used by King John, and I told Diane of its haunted reputation. I knew about its notoriety because I had made it up during the car journey there, but then again there was nothing to disprove it. The spooks must have been listening, and with a fabulous sense of humour, the bedroom window flew open in the middle of the night. The welcome result was that Diane clung to me all night.

Having children meant that we looked for hotels that had family rooms, limiting the opportunities, but with the internet, it was always possible to find somewhere suitable.

When I found climbing stairs difficult, we had to look for hotels with lifts or ground floor rooms. As the level of my disability increased so did the number of requirements. We have stayed in great hotels, but sometimes they miss the mark. On a weekend break to a country hotel, I should have twigged that the room might be approaching our worst nightmare when we were handed the keys to room 101.

Another time I had booked a couple of nights at a hotel in Southampton. It would give us a chance to relax and explore the town a little before the beginning of a cruising adventure. Some online booking systems allow you to book an accessible room, but I have phoned to confirm details like whether there are rails around the toilet. My searches found an accessible family room which would be ideal, so I called the hotel booking line. Being a chain hotel, I was put through to central reservations. The helpful young lady on the phone patiently took my details and while I waited contacted the hotel to confirm that the room was suitable and available. She reassuringly said that a lock was put on the booking with a note so that they couldn't move me to another room.

The day before our holiday I received an email to state that an accessible family room was not available and they would place us in two bedrooms. This isn't the first time this has happened. It isn't uncommon to arrive at a hotel to find that we have moved to another less than suitable room. This usually ends up with an uncomfortable standoff with the poor harried receptionist who tries to work out an acceptable solution.

I wasn't happy that even the best-made plans get changed and demanded to speak with the hotel manager. At first, he was defensive until I explained that unlike his other guests, we couldn't directly go to another hotel. The handful of accessible rooms were now all booked up. He placed us in two adjoining rooms at the original price. We met him later, and he said that he had raised this as a training issue with head office.

During that night the electricity went off. In the morning Diane went to the reception who helpfully said that breakfast had been arranged in a neighbouring hotel. Diane asked her how I was going to get downstairs as the lifts were not working. The poor receptionist went off to contact the manager for a solution, but fortunately, the power came back on. Presumably, another training issue to be raised with head office.

I quickly learned that I have to choose which battles to fight. I am sure that it would be easy to find enough worthy issues to address, but I have no intention of spending my life writing ineffectual complaint letters to businesses. Sometimes though, there is no option.

We recently stayed at a hotel in a small rural town. The rooms were expensive, more than we would usually pay but as they had the only accessible rooms for miles around there wasn't an option. Sometimes it is nice to splash out on a little luxury, but we were to find that despite being called their executive suites, luxury was in short supply. The accessible room was on the top floor. We noticed a big sign on the door of the lift stating it was not to be used in the event of fire. We had just been told that there was no staff on the premises at night, so Diane decided to ask how I was meant to get out in the event of a fire. Perhaps there was an evac chair to get me down four flights of steps. The manager stated that he thought that there was one, somewhere. Diane explained that in the event of a fire, it would help if she didn't have to search through the whole hotel. After several requests to clarify its location, he said it was probably in a cupboard on the first floor.

We decided to look at the details on the back of the door. Perhaps the night manager wasn't up to date with the hotel policies. I got the impression that their procedures hadn't been carefully thought through. In the event of a fire, the guidance told visitors to exit quietly. Really, leave quietly! Perhaps they have silent fire alarms in case they unnecessarily disturb those guests who have decided life is just not worth living as much as a good night's sleep. I knew how to make waves and get things changed, so I sent them an email. They spent a couple of minutes composing a response to the effect that they welcomed my feedback and would review procedures in light of my comments. Well, I'm sure that did the job.

We have booked cottages on the internet. It is surprising how few booking sites allow you to search for accessible rooms or properties. On a recent hunt for a place to stay by the sea, I looked at a site listing privately owned properties. I was pleased to find that that it had a search box for wheelchair-accessible properties. Looking at the list of results, I wonder whether the owners have many ideas about what people in wheelchairs need, or even in some cases what a wheelchair is. I wonder whether the website owners have sent them any criteria. I did a search, and the first property on the list was an attractive looking three-story house, with the entrance on the ground floor and a balcony on the top floor. Immediately I am dubious. The details read precisely as follows.

"'Flotsam,' as featured on Tvs 'Homes you can't afford,' overlooks the beautiful Shitterton Sands. The spacious open-plan living area on the top floor includes a Peruvian wood burner and easy cleaning wood-effect flooring. Sliding doors lead to a full-width balcony where you can appreciate the stunning smells from the sewage outlet.

The middle floor hosts two double bedrooms with balconies, a twin bedroom, 2 ensuite shower rooms and a family bathroom. On the ground floor is another twin bedroom, and utility room."

OK, I have changed a few of the words, but you get the idea. I suppose that in some way it is accessible. As far as I can make out, I would be able to access a twin bedroom, and with luck, I could pee in the sink of the utility room. If I got bored, I could even do a bit of laundry while the rest of the family eat and party on without me upstairs. I didn't show this one to Diane in case she decided she fancied the arrangement.

Tourist Information booklets are no better. I read one recently and was pleased to see a useful guide at the front about the accessible grading system for accommodation. The grades range from M1 to M3. There are two M3 Grades and a further Access Exceptional grade dependant to your level of need, there are also grades for hearing and visual impairment. Only accommodation graded M3 or Access Exceptional needs to be step-free. Unfortunately, there was no accommodation in the guide with a higher grading than M2. It would have been more helpful and save paper and time if the book left out the guide to the grading system and included in a bold font "Don't even look if you use a wheelchair, we have no accessible accommodation, Try another region."

If you are unsteady on your feet, would you choose a holiday where the floor continually moves? I'm not talking about earthquake zones, but big cruise ships. If it is a big ship with stabilisers, it actually doesn't move much as long as you avoid a big storm. Fortunately, the Captains work hard to sail around the worst weather

Modern ships are designed to be very accessible, the floors are flat without step over bulkheads. There are rooms with accessible bathrooms and plenty of room to manoeuvre a power chair.

Our first cruise was to the fjords of Norway. This was the first time that I stayed pretty much full time in my chair. There is something to be said for watching spectacular scenery passing your bed as you wake up.

Harbours are all different heights, and tide levels go up and down. Getting off or onto the ship needs a gangplank. It is quite straight forward so long as the plank is level. At each port, two unfortunate crew had drawn the short straw and had the job of guiding chairs and heaving passengers on and off the plank. If the plank was steep, they had to heave the chair onto and down the plank. At the end of the day, they had the reverse operation heaving chairs up the plank.

Most of the sights were close to the ship, sometimes there were transfer busses, but they were all very accessible.

Some historic locations have found creative solutions to make things more accessible. On a cruise to the Mediterranean, we visited Pompeii. We booked an accessible trip with an interpreter. The Romans didn't pay much attention to accessibility, but cleverly designed platforms have made many villas and much of the main street accessible. This is no mean feat when they must preserve what is there. Fortunately, the pavements are wide and smooth enough. The roads are a barrier as they are crossed by massive stepping stones. At strategic points, metal platforms have been made to contour these stones and form bridges between them, creating a relatively unobtrusive accessible path. In a number of the houses, platforms have been built that raise a metal path a few inches above the floor. As well as being accessible, it prevents wear and tear from the many thousands of visitors each day.

In Pompeii, despite the other tourists, you feel immersed in Roman life. Glimpses of the personal lives of people who lived two thousand years ago are everywhere, some humorous, some intriguing, many familiar and many tragic. There are phallic images everywhere. They are even used as direction markers, much like a sign showing a hand and pointing finger, to show the way. Asking for directions in ancient Pompeii must have been quite an experience.

CHAPTER 28

LAB RAT

Belgian Blue cattle have a unique characteristic. They have muscles on top of muscles, and they keep growing, giving them a rump that Kim Kardashian would envy. This breed with its hyper sculpted physique is obviously coveted by beef farmers. The cattle have a mutation and don't produce an enzyme called Myostatin that inhibits the development of muscles. Without Myostatins, their muscles keep growing.

It is the same mechanism for us, as we grow up, our muscles develop, but if we didn't have Myostatins when we reach adulthood, our muscles would keep growing. We would all have physiques that would make Arnold Schwarzenegger look puny. Muscles that are so big that you can't bend your limbs aren't useful.

If you have muscular dystrophy or your muscles are wasting from another condition, it might help if you could obstruct the production of Myostatins and enable muscles to grow again. This was the theory behind a significant research study. This could benefit people with several conditions, but for many technical reasons, they chose to test the drug on people with IBM.

There are others interested in this research, but not for legitimate reasons. A drug that builds muscle mass would be a new way for bodybuilders and athletes to cheat.

A drugs company called Novartis wanted to test a new Myostatin limiting drug called Bimagrumab. Tests on mice had shown that it increased muscle mass. They recruited people with Inclusion Body Myositis across the world. Half were given the drug and the other half a placebo. Recruits wouldn't know which group they were in, that is unless they started looking like the Incredible Hulk, then it would be pretty obvious.

Unfortunately, I didn't match all the qualification criteria so I wasn't able to participate in the drugs trial, but I was suitable for two accompanying studies. The first was a genetic analysis, and my involvement was donating a few millilitres of blood. For the second study, my involvement was more intensive. My first experience was to travel to London and visit the National Hospital for Neurology and Neurosurgery on Queens Square, London. I knew the area well from work I did in years gone by, but it was the first time that I had been to London in a wheelchair.

We travelled by train. Trains were not designed to be accessible. The train and the platform are at different levels. Long before modern trains, all wheelchair users were forced to travel in the guard's van, along with bikes, piles of goods and the occasional drunk thrown off the central part of the train. These days you have to arrange for someone to put out the ramp to board the train and hope that the system works and there will be another person waiting for you with a ramp when you alight. If the message doesn't get through you are stuck on the train. I haven't travelled much on trains, and the system has always worked for me, but a study by RICA, the disability and older consumers' research charity (now the RIDC), found that it worked 90% of the time. There are numerous stories of people in wheelchairs missing stops or being helpfully dragged off the train by other kind and sturdy passengers. Major new infrastructure projects are making access improvements to the stations and level access onto trains, but there is a massive antiquated network, so I expect this system will continue for some time.

Recently we went on the Luas, the Dublin tram system where I could just drive my wheelchair on and off without any thought or assistance. The step-less entry also makes it safer for children and old people, easier for people with suitcases and pushchairs and removes a tripping hazard for everyone. No one is disadvantaged apart from the few who enjoy sitting in a quiet carriage without the distraction of children, the obligation to give up their seats for old people, or the inconvenience of people with suitcases, wheelchairs and pushchairs. This is the same for Nottingham trams, and I expect for all the new tram systems in the UK, well it should be.

When we arrived at the research centre, we were warmly welcomed by one of the research team, a Polish lady who had coordinated the process. After completing an interview and several questionnaires, I was taken to a room decked out like an odd-looking gym to undertake muscle tests on my legs, arms and grip. Each experiment involved pulling against a rope or squeezing some contraption for several seconds before releasing. I then had to do a timed walking test, and this was repeated twice after short rests. The starting point was some red tape on the floor at one end of the room. I had to walk to the far strip, turn and return and repeating this for a set time. The room was small, so the walk entailed going out of the door, down a short corridor, past the toilets and into a small staff kitchen. Before I started, the researcher had to check the restrooms were unoccupied as the door opened across my path. Anyone wishing to use the toilet was quickly ushered off and directed to other facilities. I started my walk, out of the room, down the corridor and into the kitchen. At the table, three medical staff sat eating their sandwiches. We exchanged greetings as I turned for my return journey. A minute or two later, I returned, and more pleasantries were exchanged. As I returned another couple of times, I was entertained with greetings of "You again?" and "Seems we can't get rid of you".

It felt like quite a work out so I was quite pleased when the researcher said that we could go for lunch and she took us to the canteen. A session at the MRI scanner was booked in the afternoon, and so I was taken to the waiting room. As Diane wouldn't be able to come into the MRI, she was pointed in the direction of some shops.

The MRI would measure the size of my thigh muscles. It would be repeated over time to gain an accurate measurement of how much they had diminished.

A nurse took me to a cubicle and asked me to undress completely and put on a gown. I had put on a hospital gown on before, but it took me a little while to remember which way round it goes. The edges of the robe seem to have been designed not to meet up. I don't know if the lack of material is a cost -saving exercise or a joke by some bored and sadistic procurement manager. I decided which way was the more decorous option and came out of the cubicle with my bum al fresco.

I was transferred to a table. Lying on my back, I realised that I had made the right gown decision. A jigsaw of shaped pieces of foam were placed under my leg to hold it in precisely the same position each visit. Once they were satisfied, my leg was taped in place.

I waited on my table behind a screen in a quiet corridor. I assumed that it would be perhaps twenty minutes or so before someone would take me in. I had no way to measure time, and no one came down this end of the corridor. I lost track of time, and I started to wonder if I had been forgotten. One of the two MRI scanners wasn't working, and two patients needing an urgent scan naturally took priority, so there was a backlog. I had my scan and dressed. When I got back into the waiting room, Diane was there looking agitated as our return train would leave in less than 30 minutes. We said goodbye to the researcher and raced out to hail a taxi.

Fortune was on our side and the first taxi we hailed stopped. The young driver told us that he had only recently completed "The Knowledge" and a disability awareness course. When he saw that I was in a wheelchair, he was really pleased that we had hailed him. I was the first wheelchair he had taken in his cab, and he wanted to ensure that he could fit the ramp and secure the chair without any hesitation or mistakes. This was particularly timely for him as the next day he was taking his wheelchair-using future Mother in Law to the airport. I was pleased to be of help. With his help, we arrived at Euston Passenger Assist desk just in time.

Each month I had a questionnaire to complete about my falls over that period. They mainly wanted to know if I had any injuries and visits to Accident and Emergency. Throughout the research, I had an average of two falls a month which was actually an improvement on previous years.

I went back several times, once because the MRI machine failed, but as with many trials, the wonder drug failed at its first hurdle, so all the trials and the accompanying research projects were cancelled.

CHAPTER 29

AND THE WORLD COMES TUMBLING DOWN

Falls are less frequent now that I use a wheelchair, but they still happen to keep me on my toes. I literally couldn't have used a less appropriate phrase.

One problem with elbows is that you can't see them. Climbing into a house can be a risk, my foot didn't quite clear the rise and touched the step. That was just enough to throw my balance. For an instant, I saw a chance of recovery and tried to grab the doorframe. It was no benefit my knees buckled and I fell backwards. There was a scream from the door, my mother-in-law ran inside calling out "He's fallen!"

I lay on the block paved drive, and I felt lucky. Despite the unforgiving surface, my legs felt fine. I could feel that I had scraped my elbow a little and banged my fingers, but that is the sort of pain that passes quickly. Bruised fingers on my left hand are not too much of a problem, and a scraped elbow is quickly patched up.

By this time Diane had rushed from inside and was beside me. She tenderly implored me to stay still until I knew what I had done. When you fall there is a sudden mass rush of adrenalin, that can be very deceptive. It's best to stay still until a wave of pain dulls a little. If the pain is awful I start shaking uncontrollably, often I am so focused on one pain, I am totally unaware of other injuries. I assured her that I wasn't too bad, so with love she said "You idiot!" and smiled.

"How are we going to get you up?" This is the time that the Camel comes into its own. Unfortunately, it is no good left in a cupboard at home. As we set out earlier, Diane asked if we should take the Camel and I had dismissed it with "No need". Not a great decision.

Diane brought round my wheelchair, and we tried a range of different ways to get me up. Each attempt, my trousers slipped down a little. Eventually, I worked out that if we took off one of the arms, I could sort of roll onto the chair. Now, this isn't a graceful manoeuvre, I was more concerned that I was now showing my big white backside. The neighbour had recently given birth to her first child, I felt that she probably had enough on her plate without this sight.

As I finally made it onto the seat Diane pointed out that there was a lot of blood on my shirt, now there was also a lot of blood on her blouse as well. The graze on my elbow was actually a deep cut, so Diane bandaged me up. We stayed and had tea as planned, but afterwards, we decided that I better go and get stitched up.

There were few people at the walk-in centre, so we were ushered through quickly. The nurse took a look at the cut and asked a few questions. He pressed a few places around my elbow, and a few spots were a little tender. Almost as an aside, I mentioned that I had hurt my fingers a little. He pressed one of my fingers and asked if it was painful "No fine", the same for the next digit, and the next. Lastly, he pressed my thumb. "Holy mother.." followed by a string of oaths. It was a strange expletive, almost like an involuntary blasphemous prayer. Exceptionally odd as I don't go to church and have never been a catholic. It is more likely that it lodged in my mind from Father Ted. If there comes a day of judgement, I'd hope that the circumstances would be taken into consideration, after all, if HE had used some of his omnipotent powers I wouldn't have been in this situation. Come judgement day perhaps pointing this out wouldn't be the wisest approach. Profanity probably doesn't rank high on my list of past sins, so I suspect that this incident would be in an extensive file named "Other sins to be taken into consideration."

An X-ray showed that I had broken my thumb. He could splint that, but he explained that the wound in my elbow was deep and would need stitches.

On the table were a selection of packets and dressings, together with a large syringe. I assumed this was to wash the wound out. The nurse picked up the syringe and as he added a needle, explained that local anaesthetics sting. "Holy mother.." another one to be added to the list.

I chatted inanely in an attempt to distract myself "Why had we got in OWW so quickly, are Sunday evenings OOCH a quiet time to come?."

"Football" he responded. The world cup was on TV. It appears that for all their bouncing around, supporters have fewer injuries while watching football than in everyday life. I expect that it is more likely that they continue watching the game bandaged in a tea towel.

"How do you learn how to stitch people up?" I asked. The nurse explained that when he learned, they practised on the unconscious drunks brought in by the police after a fight. There was a steady supply of teaching material on an average Saturday night. Presumably, they would wake up after a hangover with a sore head and too embarrassed to complain if the stitching wasn't too tidy.

"They can't do that now though" I wondered whether this change in rules resulted from a particularly incompetent student stitching a collar onto an ear or worse. He explained that it's not seen as the right thing to do any longer.

"Now we use pigs trotters" I envisaged a waiting room full of pigs, after a long night of wild partying and following Miss Piggy arguments, line up with their drunken trotter wounds.

"At the moment though I am teaching a vegan, and she can't touch trotters, so we have to use sponges instead. It's not like real flesh" the nurse continued "Actually, I really enjoy stitching people up, it's the favourite part of my job" Tactlessly I enquire whether it satisfied a small sadistic streak. This was a foolish question, especially as he was still stitching. He ignored me and carried on. "It's because I like putting people back together again, they come in broken, and we mend them."

My elbow was bandaged up and thumb supported in a sticking plaster splint. I left, thanking the nurse and with an appointment for the fracture clinic the following day.

I sat on my wheelchair in the clinic waiting room. I can't figure out why so many Hospital waiting areas get things so wrong. If someone who arranged the seats had thought to try getting around using a wheelchair or with crutches they might have some idea of the problems they have created. No waiting room is the same, and there is no uniform hospital chair, some with arms and some without. If there were no chairs with arms, I wouldn't be able to get up again if I sat down, so I stand. If there were chairs with arms, I have to judge whether they are strong enough. The way I stand up is to lift my full bodyweight using my arms. Less substantial chairs start to bend as I get up. Breaking the arms off the waiting room chair would ensure that I was remembered.

Most waiting areas now have chairs for the overweight and extra-wide chairs that look a little like small sofas. I admire the fact that corpulent people have fought for the right to have comfortable seating. Perhaps those of us who have difficulty getting to their feet should stand up for our rights, or at least try to stand up.

Now that I use a wheelchair, I don't have the worry of getting up, but there is now another problem, where to park the wheelchair. Very few waiting rooms have left spaces for wheelchairs. If I'm lucky, I will be able to park relatively tidily at the end of a row. Porters wheeling patients in chairs know the best places to park but often the only option they have is to park them next to a door or in a corridor, getting in the way of staff. Hasn't anyone realised that quite a lot of patients use wheelchairs?

In this waiting room, someone had worked out how to fit the maximum possible chairs. There were possibly fifty seats in total. Those with casts sat on the front seats. Pedestrians and wheelchairs would give a full birth and wait for traffic coming in the other direction. When a bed is brought through, like synchronised swimmers, their plastered limbs move to the side. Those on crutches or with sticks, awkwardly file sideways down the aisles between the chairs. One open space was left for a wheelchair. This was filled, so I had to find a spot to wait along the corridor. As four other wheelchair users were already filling all available space, the only option was to park at the end of the aisle and for Diane to wheel me out whenever anyone needed to pass.

It is a modern hospital, and there are automatic doors in many places. Someone decided that here it would be an unnecessary expense. Presumably assuming most would be able to lever open the heavy doors with their with crutches, or those in wheelchairs could use their cast leg to ram the gates open. Every few minutes we would watch someone struggle to get in or out.

I think the purpose of the clinic was to review what the nurses had done the previous day. Judging by the seconds I spent with the doctor, they must have done a pretty good job. I was sent to the fracture room to get a new, more permanent splint and a fresh dressing.

I have got particularly hairy hands, and the plaster strips were surprisingly sticky. "This will hurt a bit" the nurse explained, "Do you want me to pull it in one go."

Something I have never tried, but I have always thought that people who have their legs waxed tend to make a bit of unnecessary fuss, so I replied,

"Yes, go for it!"

Incorrectly I assumed that I would have a little time to mentally prepare myself.

"Ahh, Holy...." and another sin for consideration

Diane said that she should drive home. She doesn't like driving my car and so was persuaded that I was fit to drive home, carefully. Driving wasn't a problem, no need to use either my left thumb or elbow. By the time I went to bed, I felt things had gone well. After all, if I was to injure my body, I couldn't have chosen two less useful appendages. Although uncomfortable, there was nothing these injuries prevented me from doing and I eventually get to sleep.

At three o'clock, I really need the toilet, and I am lying in bed realising that I use both my elbow and thumb to push myself up.

It is an unfortunate reality that you are mostly unaware of your own body odours. Miss a shower, and it isn't you who suffers. Miss twenty and quite possibly you would still be unaware until you notice that no one visits any longer, people giving you more room when you are out, and the retching sound when someone accidentally gets too close. Regular baths or showers supported with the masking effects of body sprays, deodorants and aftershaves are your only hope of avoiding offending the olfactory senses of others.

My hand splint was a different matter. It was constructed of nylon coated neoprene, so in effect, it was a fingerless wetsuit mitten. Like a wetsuit, the neoprene is a fantastic insulator from the freezing seawater and a thin film of seawater slowly flushes through regulating your temperature. As a splint however, the neoprene still insulates so that the inside rises to oven temperatures. In turn, this draws a constant stream of sweat from the covered skin. After half a day you get an occasional whiff of a distinctive but unplaceable smell. When you later remove the splint to wash your hand, you can't believe the strength of the odour, so you thoroughly clean your hand and splint. This continues each day, but by day two, the smell remains when you wash the splint. By day five, the smell remains when you wash your hand, even a scourer and washing up liquid makes no difference. The odour is like nothing you have smelt before. I have no experience of this but imagine it is similar to the smell that would emanate from the opening of an exhumed coffin.

After six weeks, I had an appointment to go back to the fracture clinic. My thumb was beautiful, and the bone had long healed, and I could move it as well as I did previously.

CHAPTER 30

THE FUTURE

The future looks bleak. I don't mean for me, I mean for all of us. After all, we are all in a long queue waiting until it is our turn to shake hands with the Grim Reaper. That is assuming that we all don't bow out at the same time after a meteorite crashes into the earth. Not that we can do much about it.

The first thing to realise is that we are fortunate just to be here at all. As a point of fact almost mindbogglingly lucky.

There are 100 billion trillion stars in the observable universe. That's just the observable universe, goodness knows how many planets there are. Whatever it is that makes you you, happens to be on the only world that we know to contain life. So the first piece of good luck is that you here and not some rock or weird alien life form on a lonely bleak planet on the far side of Alpa Sentori.

Add to that, life has existed on Earth for about 3.5 billion years. Imagine this timeline being like a giant sparkler, a really, really big sparkler, in fact long enough to reach the moon. Each living thing is a spark that comes and goes in a 10th of a second. The first sparks were lit in some primordial soup. Initially the sparkler it wasn't very bright, but it has gradually built intensity. There are a lot of living things. If you add up every cow, chicken and ant, there would be currently perhaps 20 billion, billion sparks. You are one of those sparks, and your light is shining at this moment, so enjoy it. The chances of all the constituents that make up you being on earth, of you being alive at this present time and being human are vanishingly small, about 1 chance in 10 followed by a million zeros or the same probability as your cat bringing you a gift of something more delightful than a dead mouse. Actually, I have no idea what the figure is, I just made it up, but it is very, very small.

If you compare your unbelievable luck in getting this far your chances of winning a lottery jackpot seem like a comparative certainty.

When I was young, magpies were not quite as prevalent as they are now. Like the rest of my family, I was the opposite of superstitious, but I knew the rhyme, "one for sorrow, two for joy, three for a girl and four for a boy..." Despite my cynicism, seeing a solitary magpie perched above the doorway as I entered an exam, or as I approached a first date, wouldn't give me a feeling of comfort and reassurance. This all changed when I was told something very wise, it wasn't from an old guru reclusively sitting on his mountain top, but from a stranger, although perhaps they had heard it from a guru.

"Magpies always come in pairs. Sometimes it can take days or even weeks before you see the other half of the pair, but they are always there."

This is true, it's a fact, look for yourself. Another fact about magpie pairs is that they don't even need to be in the same area. You could see a magpie in London, fly to Australia and its pair would be somewhere there. This is particularly amazing because the Australian magpies are a different species. I don't even bother to look for the other half of the pair, if I see a magpie, of which there are many, then I know that it's my lucky day.

Saint Fillan was a man who knew that magpies come in pairs. He found a unique advantage in his impairment. On the Fife coast is a beautiful fishing village called Pittenween. We stayed there once, and it is well worth a visit. We enjoyed watching harbour seals hoping for an easy meal from returning fishing boats. Fillan lived in a hermits cave in the middle of the village. It is a comfortable size and dry. Fillan's unique impairment must have received some inquisitive stares especially at night, but in the cave, his impairment became a definite advantage. He had an arm that glowed. When Fillian had lived in a monastery, the light would disturb the sleep of the other monks in a dormitory, which is presumably why he lived as a hermit. But it was useful for cave living, and Fillan's arm was bright enough that he could read and write his sacred scriptures.

Just having an incandescent arm, however, is not enough to get you a sainthood, so Fillan set to work using its mystical powers to heal the mentally ill. It can't have been easy to explain to his patients that they had been completely cured of delusions by a man with an arm like a torch who lives in a hole in the ground. The spiritual glow was possibly had a more down to earth cause, a bacterial infection condition called Erythrasma. Well, this is a less romantic version according to something I read on the internet. These days your best chances of seeing a glowing arm would be swimmers on the beaches of Sellafield.

There is a fair chance that someday they will find a cure for IBM, which would be amazing. I notice that people with incurable conditions are often eager to be involved in research even when it is unlikely to help them. There is an innate desire to improve things for future generations. I would love to see a cure, but as my muscles are increasingly wasted, it is unlikely to benefit me. I am also sure that access and technology will generally improve as it has done until now.

I am in a wheelchair, I am not able to do lots of the things I loved doing, I have had depression, and I know that my condition is progressive, but I am so lucky.

I hope you enjoyed the book

Please rate or recommend
"Up Cripple Creek"
on Goodreads

or

review the book on
Amazon or the online
store of purchase.

Have you written a book?

I am keen to work in collaboration with
anyone who has written an unusual or
humorous memoir or story and would like
to publish and sell their book.

Please contact me at
www.facebook.com/wobblymanpress
with a brief summary.